The Path to Profitable Measures

10 Steps to Feedback That Fuels Performance

Also available from ASQ Quality Press:

From Quality to Business Excellence: A Systems Approach
to Management
Charles G. Cobb

Mapping Work Processes
Dianne Galloway

Office Kaizen: Transforming Office Operations into a Strategic
Competitive Advantage
William Lareau

Business Process Improvement Toolbox
Bjørn Andersen and Tom Fagerhaug

Root Cause Analysis: Simplified Tools and Techniques
Bjørn Andersen and Tom Fagerhaug

Principles and Practices of Organizational Performance Excellence
Thomas J. Cartin

Defining and Analyzing a Business Process: A Six Sigma Pocket Guide
Jeffrey N. Lowenthal

Six Sigma Project Management: A Pocket Guide
Jeffrey N. Lowenthal

Customer Centered Six Sigma: Linking Customers, Process Improvement,
and Financial Results
Earl Naumann and Steven H. Hoisington

The Change Agent's Guide to Radical Improvement
Ken Miller

The Certified Quality Manager Handbook, Second Edition
Duke Okes and Russell T. Westcott, editors

To request a complimentary catalog of ASQ Quality Press publications,
call 800-248-1946, or visit our Web site at http://qualitypress.asq.org.

The Path to Profitable Measures

10 Steps to Feedback That Fuels Performance

Mark W. Morgan

"AMERICAN SOCIETY FOR QUALITY - QIC"

ASQ Quality Press
Milwaukee, Wisconsin

American Society for Quality, Quality Press, Milwaukee 53203
© 2005 by ASQ
All rights reserved. Published 2005
Printed in the United States of America

12 11 10 09 08 07 06 05   5 4 3 2 1

Library of Congress Cataloging-in-Publication Data

Morgan, Mark W.
   The path to profitable measures : 10 steps to feedback that fuels
performance / Mark W. Morgan.
     p. cm.
   Includes bibliographical references and index.
   ISBN 0-87389-649-1 (soft cover, perfect bound : alk. paper)
   1. Management audit. 2. Organizational effectiveness—Measurement.
3. Performance technology. I. Title.

   HD58.95.M67 2005
   658.4'013—dc22   2005002128

ISBN 0-87389-649-1

Publisher: William A. Tony
Acquisitions Editor: Annemieke Hytinen
Project Editor: Paul O'Mara
Production Administrator: Randall Benson

ASQ Mission: The American Society for Quality advances individual,
organizational, and community excellence worldwide through learning,
quality improvement, and knowledge exchange.

Attention Bookstores, Wholesalers, Schools, and Corporations: ASQ Quality
Press books, videotapes, audiotapes, and software are available at quantity
discounts with bulk purchases for business, educational, or instructional use.
For information, please contact ASQ Quality Press at 800-248-1946, or write to
ASQ Quality Press, P.O. Box 3005, Milwaukee, WI 53201-3005.

To place orders or to request a free copy of the ASQ Quality Press Publications
Catalog, including ASQ membership information, call 800-248-1946. Visit our
Web site at www.asq.org or http://qualitypress.asq.org.

∞ Printed on acid-free paper

Quality Press
600 N. Plankinton Avenue
Milwaukee, Wisconsin 53203
Call toll free 800-248-1946
Fax 414-272-1734
www.asq.org
http://qualitypress.asq.org
http://standardsgroup.asq.org
E-mail: authors@asq.org

Contents

List of Figures

Introduction

As an executive coach, working with thousands of managers from hundreds of organizations over the past 25 years, helping them improve feedback, performance, and results, I quickly discovered that most managers suffer from data glut and information famine. The constant stream of reports, e-mails, phone calls, and meetings usually fails to provide the feedback busy people need to make rapid and meaningful decisions.

Most managers would love to cut through the clutter and see performance outcomes. They are, however, usually victims of information systems that have evolved over time without careful thought. The result is floods of reports and reviews—with trickles of meaningful information and useful feedback.

Using this book, you will apply 10 simple steps to turn your information flood into meaningful feedback for you and your work team. Together we will identify the critical measures that you and your team need to monitor to achieve business goals with less time, stress, and cost.

When developed properly, good feedback helps you and your team achieve better alignment, visibility, and communication. Good measures form the foundation of feedback that helps you evaluate performance and sustain progress.

Every manager has a unique set of measures matched to his or her goals and responsibilities. As a leader, you must think through and define the correct set of indicators for your needs.

In other words, you must design and tailor this unique set of indicators—your *Scorecard*—to match your goals and responsibilities. No one else will have a Scorecard exactly the same as yours.

So we are going to develop and use your Scorecard, leading to better feedback—and better business results. Enjoy the 10 steps, and contact me at any point with questions. Let's get started!

What is a
Scorecard?

In simple terms, a Scorecard is the complete set of measures necessary to monitor and improve business results. A Scorecard graphically and visually displays results in such a way that you can easily see whether you are progressing toward targets.

Scorecards take reams of reports and distill them into simple, easy-to-interpret charts. Usually Scorecards have a limited set of measures—about six to 20 indicators—that provide the essential information you need to know. Generally, Scorecards organize the measures into categories that align with strategic goals.

Every manager should have a Scorecard. A manager is anyone with responsibility for budgets and business targets. This includes everyone from the CEO to a department supervisor.

You should have a Scorecard—and probably have the rudiments of a Scorecard now. However, if you're like most managers, your Scorecard is scattered, poorly designed, and inadequate for the myriad of decisions you must make.

Your Scorecard is unique, yet linked to customers' requirements, suppliers' inputs, strategic goals, and your work team's results. Using this book, we will develop your Scorecard.

Ultimately, you want each manager in your organization to develop and use his or her unique, yet linked, Scorecard. However, linking Scorecards throughout an organization is a large undertaking and is beyond the scope of this book. In the Suggested Readings section of the book, I list several resources that provide instructions and illustrations for linking Scorecards, a significant task for most organizations. However, you don't need to link Scorecards to begin realizing the advantages of better measures and enhanced feedback.

For the 10 steps defined in this book, we will focus on defining and developing your Scorecard with measures that fit you and enable you to apply better feedback.

What does a Scorecard look like?

A sample Scorecard is provided in Figure 1. Formats vary across organizations, but good Scorecards use graphics and charts to tell the story of performance at a glance.

Scorecards provide an indication of past performance, current performance trends, and performance relative to meaningful targets. Scorecard charts provide clear, consistent feedback to managers to enable decision making and appropriate actions.

Scorecards avoid mind-numbing and difficult-to-interpret tables and columns of numbers. Scorecards promote discussions and understanding of *where you are* and *what you do next*.

Why should I use a Scorecard?

Your Scorecard has one primary purpose: to help you improve business results.

Properly designed, your Scorecard tells you whether you are generating sufficient revenues, profits, and financial returns. Your Scorecard gives you feedback on whether customers are willing to give you repeat business.

Your Scorecard will help you evaluate whether your operation is performing well and generating value-producing outcomes with minimal costs and

**To the Moon, Inc.
Executive Scorecard**

Priority goals:
- Increase revenues to $4.0M
- Achieve market leadership of 42%
- Earn customer loyalty of 90
- Achieve employee ratings of 75
- Increase operations yields by 10%

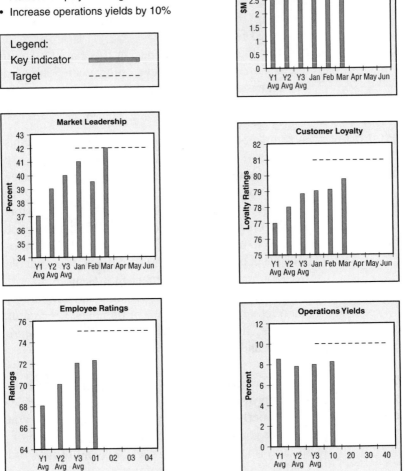

Figure 1 A sample top-level executive Scorecard.

waste. Additionally, your Scorecard gives you indications that employees are productive and planning to stick around.

With just a few carefully selected indicators, your Scorecard will tell you, at a glance, whether you are winning or losing. You can make rapid, timely decisions on where to invest your time and resources to achieve needed gains.

What will we do in the 10 steps?

Here's a quick overview of our 10 steps to better feedback:

1. *Assess your measures.* We'll make sure the remaining nine steps are worth your while.

2. *Identify long-term outcomes.* From strategic plans, we'll identify the essential categories that your Scorecard must include.

3. *Develop your goals.* We'll define or tweak your goals that easily align and translate into better feedback.

4. *Define your finance indicators.* We'll develop the best financial indicators for your responsibilities.

5. *Define your customer indicators.* We'll pinpoint the two or three customer indicators you need to know.

6. *Determine your operations indicators.* Together, we define the right measures that will give you a window into your work processes and your abilities to deliver results that keep customers coming back.

7. *Determine your employee indicators.* We'll identify and use the essential employee indicators.

8. *Mature your measures.* I'll walk you through ways to use your feedback effectively, know what to watch, and determine when to take action.

9. *Set inspiring targets.* Bad targets are a team turnoff. I'll help you set targets at levels that keep your team energized and focused.

10. *Boost results.* We'll use measures and better feedback to spark desired outcomes and spur continuous performance improvements. Plus, you'll save time and materials by quickly reviewing reports, identifying issues, and fixing recurring problems.

My title is manager, but I don't have any employees reporting to me. Do I need a Scorecard?

Absolutely! In fact, a Scorecard will help you immensely, as it will highlight your individual contributions to your organization.

If you are one of the special breed of managers serving as an individual contributor, staff manager, or other role without any direct reports, your Scorecard will help you in discussions with your boss to clarify your role, assess your performance, and demonstrate your unique value.

How long will this take?

The time to complete the 10 steps varies according to your motivation and willingness to apply these lessons. Most people, devoting an hour a day to studying and applying these lessons, will start seeing better measures within a week.

Within a month, communication and feedback will improve. Within three months, most people start to experience better results—with more significant gains within the year.

Your Scorecard continuously evolves as your business changes. You should regularly reapply these lessons to keep your measures relevant as your business grows and your needs change.

*What will
I gain?*

You will more easily:

- Identify and eliminate waste and inefficiency.

- Find and eliminate bottlenecks in your work flows.

- Understand what customers really want and ensure that you are meeting their needs and building loyalty and repeat business.

- Help employees see how they contribute to the business, and use feedback to continuously improve their results.

- Promote accountability and action within your team.

- Relate and connect the elements in the value chain, leading to greater gains with less effort.

You begin to understand how to use measures to achieve desired outcomes. You will eliminate obsolete measures and reduce cost overhead associated with tracking information no one wants.

You set targets that make sense to your customers and employees. You help everyone understand how efforts align with results. Most importantly, you gain back some of your most valuable resources—your time, energy, and attention.

*What's
different
about this
book?*

Most books on performance measurement tell you the benefits of Scorecards, but leave you wondering how to develop better measures. With this book, you will develop and begin using your Scorecard to improve feedback and performance.

This book is designed for busy managers who wish to improve the performance of their teams and organizations using better measures and feedback. The book is straightforward and uncomplicated, with no difficult jargon. No background knowledge of quality management, statistics, or mathematics is required. All managers, regardless of industry, organization, or level, can apply the step-by-step approach.

Each step in the book is illustrated with examples to help you understand and apply the approach immediately. We will not spend much time on the theory or rationale for scorecards covered in other books; I know from experience with hundreds of executives that better measures, used properly, lead to better results. My aim is to give you something that works and makes your life and role as a leader easier and more rewarding.

How do I get started?

You've already started by reading this far! In this book, I will walk you through the 10 steps to better measures and help you develop your Scorecard.

As a result, you will have better visibility on progress toward your goals, fewer anxieties from wondering if you're doing the right things, and better tools for communicating progress to your boss, your team, and other stakeholders.

Most people think that this will result in more work, more reports, and more hassles. Actually, the opposite is true.

Leading organizations and top-tier managers spend less time reviewing fewer measures— because they took the time to define the right set of measures. They eliminated the tons of measures that don't mean a thing, saving time and resources.

So let's get started with Step 1: Assess Your Measures.

Step 1:
Assess Your Measures

What do I do?

I'm sure that you have some measures for monitoring business performance already. We don't want to throw everything out and start over—let's see what you've got!

The following assessment is one that I frequently use with managers to gain insight into their indicators. It is not a scientific instrument, just one developed over time to help clients determine a starting point.

The assessment explores three areas: how well your feedback aligns with strategy; how well your measures provide timely and meaningful feedback; and whether your Scorecard content is effective and useful.

Take a few moments to complete the following assessment to determine how well your current practices are delivering the right feedback to you and your team.

Finally, determine how well your current measures—and Scorecard—are meeting your needs.

If you find that your score is sufficiently high and that you really don't need to improve your measures and feedback, box this book up and return it for a full refund.

If there's a possibility that you just might benefit from better measures and feedback, continue with the lessons and enjoy the improved outcomes.

Section A: Aligning Measures With Strategy

Read each of the following statements. For each statement, rate your perception of how well your current measures align with your organization's strategies and long-term goals. Use the following scale:

5 = Excellent

4 = Very good

3 = Good

2 = Fair

1 = Poor

Section A: Aligning Measures with Strategy	Rating (5 to 1)
My organization's strategic plan (or top-level business plan) has been developed or updated within the past 12 months.	
Our strategic plan provides clear long-term goals, strategies to achieve those goals, and short-term milestones and goals.	
Top-level indicators for evaluating strategic plan progress are tracked by our senior executives.	
The strategic plan was communicated in such a way that I know what to do to contribute to long-term goals.	
I understand how I contribute to the top-level goals defined in the strategic plan.	
My business unit's plans and goals are directly linked to the strategic plan.	
My measures are directly linked to the strategic plan and my business goals.	
My business unit's targets are directly linked to the strategies and goals of the strategic plan.	
Goals for my team are linked to the strategic plan.	
My employees can tell you the key elements of our strategic plan.	
Subtotal	

Section B: Measurement Processes

Read each of the following statements. For each statement, rate your perception of how well your entire organization captures and uses measures effectively to monitor results. Use the following scale:

5 = Excellent

4 = Very good

3 = Good

2 = Fair

1 = Poor

Section B: Measurement Processes	Rating (5 to 1)
My measures are tailored to match my business goals and responsibilities.	
I am accountable for measurement accuracy and results.	
I regularly review results with the right measures and the right people.	
My reviews focus on constructive discussions of actions for improving results.	
Following our reviews, actions are taken to improve measures and results.	
Compensation and incentives are tied to measurement results.	
I integrate measures with our work flows, allowing me to spot process problems and track outcomes.	
I ensure that measurement information is protected and valid.	
I include employees in reviews and feedback cycles to help them link efforts with results.	
I regularly review our measures to ensure that they are appropriate for our goals, responsibilities, and customers' expectations.	
Subtotal	

Section C: Scorecard Content

Read each of the following statements. For each statement, rate your perception of how well your entire organization presents and acts on measurement information to improve results. Use the following scale:

5 = Excellent

4 = Very good

3 = Good

$2 = $ Fair

$1 = $ Poor

Section C: Measurement Content	Rating (5 to 1)
My measures monitor and evaluate progress toward my key business goals.	
My measures provide important information that helps me make decisions and take actions to improve results.	
My measures provide a balance for monitoring results in important areas such as finances, customers, processes, and employees.	
Historical trends, current levels, and desired targets are clear for each of my measures.	
With a quick glance at my measures, I can tell where I need to focus time and resources to achieve gains.	
I can translate actions into results (that is, when my team and I take positive action, we see the outcome in our measures).	
My measures provide a clear picture of how well my processes are working to generate value and customer fulfillment.	
I can quantify and link relationships between my measures (for example, I can predict changes in revenues from changes in operational results).	
My measures and targets are linked to customers' and market expectations.	
My measures report honest and accurate results.	
Subtotal	

Score Your Results

Total your scores from each section. Then, multiply your section scores by the appropriate multiplier ($\times 3$ for strategy, $\times 2$ for processes, $\times 1$ for content). Total your multiplied scores.

Assessment Section	Score	Multiplier	Multiplied Score
A: Aligning Measures with Strategy		× 3	
B: Measurement Processes		× 2	
C: Measurement Content		× 1	
		Assessment Total	

How do I interpret my results?

300 to 270. Excellent! Call me, as I can use your expertise and examples to show others how to create better feedback! You are enjoying the fruits of wonderful measures and terrific feedback.

269 to 240. Pretty good! You may want to review some of the lessons to sharpen your measures, but you are on the right trail. Keep going!

239 to 180. You have many of the right indicators and practices, but haven't connected all of the elements yet. Keep reading and working the exercises. You can really benefit from better feedback.

179 to 100. Believe it or not, you are in the majority of executives. Keep going with the remaining nine steps. A whole world of better performance with less hassle is waiting for you.

99 to 60. Close your book, say a prayer of thanks that you found someone to help, and call me immediately. You are going to need more help than this book provides.

Good job completing the assessment. Continue your path to improved measures by moving on to Step 2—and more profitable feedback!

Step 2:
Identify Long-Term Outcomes

Introduction If your organization is like most, you experience three problems:

- Your strategic plan is nonexistent or gathering dust.

- You find it difficult to sustain efforts toward long-term results.

- You feel that your employees' efforts toward strategic goals are scattered or misdirected.

In 2004, *Fortune* magazine noted that leading companies execute their business strategies better than other companies due to the presence of seven essential elements:

- Well-established business functions

- Strategies with action plans and accountability

- Clear roles and responsibilities

- Well-defined decision-making processes

- Leaders willing to listen

- Good talent

- Performance measures directly tied to business goals[1]

Scorecards are only one element of a successful organization, but an essential element that forms the foundation for decision making, action, and achievement of business goals.

Often, I have seen companies and leaders unable to execute strategies because measures and performance systems were out of alignment. Nothing seemed to work well in the organization—including capable talent—because no one knew what was really going on.

As you develop your Scorecard, you will begin to bring these systems into alignment and see consistency of efforts and results. By clarifying your intent, communicating measurable expectations, and providing actionable feedback, your Scorecard helps you streamline your path toward results.

As you begin developing your Scorecard, you want to make sure that your measures are consistent and aligned with long-term plans. In this step, we will walk through a review of your organization's strategic plan and tell you what to look for.

By the way, if your organization does not have or your boss is unable or unwilling to provide you with a strategic plan, jump to Step 3, Develop Your Goals. You can develop a "stand-alone" Scorecard based on your specific goals, though it would be more effective if aligned with top-level goals.

How does my organization's strategic plan relate to my Scorecard?

A long-term plan is important as you build a Scorecard, because your Scorecard must align with plans and goals. A Scorecard is simply a tool for helping you achieve goals by:

- Communicating goals and intent

- Clarifying strategies

- Helping you translate the plan into operational terms and behaviors

- Breaking the plan down into measurable, bite-sized components

- Enhancing the ability to look ahead to anticipate issues and obstacles

- Pinpointing key attributes of performance

- Providing feedback on the effectiveness of the plan

- Checking on progress toward goals

Your organization probably has a long-term or strategic plan outlining goals and strategies for three to five years into the future. Get the plan from your boss or the appropriate source.

If your organization does not have a strategic plan, but wants or needs one, contact an appropriate resource. The steps in developing a strategic plan are beyond the range of this book. It's important to have long-term aims to consistently align daily efforts and clarify where your leadership team wants to go.

OK, I have the plan. What should I look for?

Study the strategic plan for a few minutes. Strategic plans vary in their depth of analysis and detail, but you should be able to find:

- The long-term vision and mission of your organization

- Your organization's strengths and competitive advantages

- The major categories of intended outcomes

- Aims or long-term goals in each category

- Strategies for achieving the aims

- Priority actions or short-term wins to build momentum toward long-term goals

What are the parts of the plan that I need?

Your strategic plan probably includes a lot of information that is not meaningful or relevant to you. Other parts, however, are speaking directly to your role and contribution to the organization. Try to identify the following:

- What are the categories for results?

- What are the values, aims, or important outcomes?

- What top-level measures or indicators are defined?

- What targets are established?

As you identify each of these, answer the following questions:

- Which goals apply to me?

- Which goals or targets do I influence?

- What's my part in achieving the goals?

Specifically, what do I need?

The main things you are looking for are the categories of intended outcomes of the organization. I have seen these called *values, key goals, dimensions,* and other terms. However, nearly every organization has four categories of outcomes:

- Finances

- Customers

- Operations

- Employees

Depending on your organization, you may have more categories, such as *regulatory compliance, community involvement, business partnerships, innovation,* or others. Identify the categories for your organization. If your organization does not have specifically defined categories (or lacks a strategic or long-term plan), use the four categories listed above—you can't go wrong.

The categories you identify should be stable and permanent—regardless of how you organize, what you sell, or how you arrange your accounts. In other words, no matter how you shuffle the deck organizationally, you must produce outcomes in these categories (*finances, customers, operations,* and *employees*).

Ultimately, you want to see the causal link between the categories. You probably already have an intuitive feel for this relationship:

Skilled employees produce *effective operations* that produce *loyal customers* that produce *financial success.*

However, many managers and organizations struggle with connecting these essential performance elements. Your Scorecard and improved feedback will help you clarify and strengthen the relationships and results in these areas.

Our Case Study

Kathy is the director of marketing for a television station in a mid-sized city. Kathy was promoted to her job nearly a year ago, and has been struggling to get her team of four employees enthused and involved.

Kathy enjoys her job and wants to do well for the station and for her boss, Robert, the station manager. She likes working for Robert, but Kathy feels that he provides very little guidance and feedback, mostly because he is extremely busy.

Kathy understands the results she and her marketing team need to produce: create a positive awareness of the station in the viewing area and attract more viewers and sponsors.

While she doesn't have direct responsibility for revenues and sales, she understands that the efforts of her team lead to ad revenues sparked by additional viewers. So her marketing efforts lead to important outcomes for Robert and the station staff.

Immediately after her promotion to marketing director—she worked in the department for three years as a marketing specialist—Kathy participated in the development of the station's three-year strategic plan. The plan was distributed to all managers, but no one has ever referred to the plan since its development.

Kathy pulled her dusty copy of the strategic plan from her bookshelf. As she examined the plan, she identified four categories of outcomes with two or three long-term goals per category.

Finances

- *Increase net revenues.*

- *Develop recurring revenue streams.*

- *Improve profits.*

Customers

- *Increase market share.*

- *Broaden diversity of viewers.*

- *Establish a distinct identity in the market.*

Operations

- *Lower operations costs by 10 percent.*

- *Ensure uniformity of branding in all on-air and off-air activities.*

Employees

- *Ensure staff is cross-trained and fully proficient in all on-air production capabilities.*

- *Increase ROI for training.*

Kathy transferred the strategic categories and long-term goals to her Path to Profitable Measures worksheet (found in the appendix on page 103), as shown in Figure 2.

Your Instructions

Summarize your organization's long-term goals on your own Path to Profitable Measures worksheet. Or set up a similar worksheet and plug in your specific categories and long-term goals.

That's it—proceed to Step 3!

Categories	Station's Long-Term Goals	Kathy's Goals	Kathy's Measures
Finances	Increase net revenues		
	Develop recurring revenue streams		
	Improve profits		
Customers	Increase market share		
	Broaden diversity of viewers		
	Establish a distinct identity in the market		
Operations	Lower operations costs		
	Ensure uniformity of branding in all on-air and off-air activities		
Employees	Ensure staff is cross-trained and fully proficient in all on-air production capabilities		
	Increase ROI for training		

Figure 2   Kathy's worksheet with the station's strategic goals.

Step 3:
Develop Your Goals

Introduction   Your Scorecard is your best tool for helping you improve business performance to achieve your goals. If you don't have any goals, you don't need a Scorecard!

In this step, we will examine, refine, and tweak your goals to establish the foundation for your Scorecard measures and better feedback.

What do I do with my annual goals?   List your annual goals or objectives. If you don't have any goals, this is the perfect opportunity to develop them!

Note: Some organizations distinguish between goals and objectives, while others do not differentiate the terms. Because the terms are inconsistent across businesses, I will use the generic term *goals* to describe statements of intended business outcomes at all levels.

Consider your goals carefully. Use the SMART rule to evaluate and refine your goals:

S: Is the goal *specific?*

M: Is the goal *measurable?*

A: Is the goal *applicable* to me?

R: Is the goal *realistic?*

T: Does the goal specify a *time* interval?

Refine your goals before you draft your Scorecard. Clearly stated goals will help you draft an effective, meaningful Scorecard.

Transfer your goals to your Path to Profitable Measures worksheet.

Our Case Study   Kathy, our fictitious marketing director, pulled her annual goals from her desk drawer. She realized that she had not even looked at them since she gave them to her boss four months ago!

Kathy's annual goals included:

- *Add new sponsors.*

- *Maintain spending within approved budget.*

- *Reach a greater audience within the station's viewing area.*

- *Host at least four special events to publicize and promote the station.*

- *Participate on the station's identity committee and promote a consistent on-air and off-air identity.*

- *Develop and distribute new marketing collateral.*

- *Have employees complete at least 24 hours of training.*

Kathy felt that these did not fit the SMART guidelines very well, so she rewrote her goals as follows:

- *Attract at least six new sponsors and retain at least 90 percent of existing sponsors by December 31.*

- *By December 31, keep department expenses within budget.*

- *Increase viewer participation in call-in shows by 10 percent by December 31.*

- *Host four public-relations events for at least 2500 participants by September 30.*

- *Develop branding identity standards guidelines and evaluate station's efforts at maintaining standards by November 30.*

- *Distribute at least 10,000 pieces of marketing collateral consistent with branding guidelines by December 31.*

- *Have employees complete 24 hours of training by August 31.*

- *Evaluate benefits from training by December 31.*

Once Kathy was satisfied with her department goals, she reexamined the station's strategic goals to check for consistency. Kathy wrote her goals on the worksheet, noting that all of her goals matched at least one strategic goal.

From her worksheet, summarized in Figure 3, Kathy also noted that she did not have department goals for some strategic goals. But the strategic goals without matching department goals appeared to be outside her area of responsibility, such as *develop recurring revenue streams.*

Satisfied with her department goals and the match with the station's strategic goals, Kathy jotted herself a note to contact Robert to discuss her restated department goals and proceeded to Step 4, Define Your Financial Indicators.

Your Instructions   Transfer your goals to your Path to Profitable Measures worksheet or to your customized worksheet. Update and refine your goals, as needed, to match the SMART guidelines.

Proceed to Step 4!

Categories	Station's Long-Term Goals	Kathy's Goals	Kathy's Measures
Finances	Increase net revenues	Attract at least six new sponsors and retain at least 90 percent of existing sponsors by December 31	
	Develop recurring revenue streams		
	Improve profits	By December 31, keep department expenses within budget	
Customers	Increase market share	Increase viewer participation in call-in shows by 10 percent by December 31	
	Broaden diversity of viewers	Host four public-relations events for at least 2500 participants by September 30	
	Establish a distinct identity in the market	Develop branding identity standards guidelines and evaluate station's efforts at maintaining standards by November 30	
Operations	Lower operations costs		
	Ensure uniformity of branding in all on-air and off-air activities	Distribute at least 10,000 pieces of marketing collateral consistent with branding guidelines by December 31	
Employees	Ensure staff is cross-trained and fully proficient in all on-air production capabilities	Have employees complete 24 hours of training by August 31	
	Increase ROI for training	Evaluate benefits from training by December 31	

Figure 3   Kathy's worksheet with her department goals.

Step 4:
Define Your Financial Indicators

Introduction

This is exciting—you're ready to define your first Scorecard measures! You can do this alone or with your work team. Either way, set aside about four hours to complete steps 4 through 7. You can accomplish this in one long meeting or in a series of short meetings. The important thing is to keep going!

Your desired outcome is a draft of the measures that will be on your Scorecard and the action plan for Step 8, Mature Your Measures.

In this step, we'll focus on the best financial indicators for your Scorecard.

Review Your Financial Goals

Every organization is concerned with the bottom line, measuring revenues, expenses, and profits. Even nonprofit organizations must match revenues with expenses, so they benefit from Scorecards, as well.

Depending on your role and level within your organization, you may have budget responsibility, revenue responsibility, and a host of other financial concerns.

Many executives, however, are flooded with a host of financial measures that mean little to them. I once worked with an organization where every executive had responsibility for "performance income"—and not a single person could explain what performance income was!

Your Scorecard must reflect the outcomes you own and control. From your goals identified in step 3, focus on those in the Finance category.

Identify Measures for Each Financial Goal

Using your Path to Profitable Measures worksheet, identify the measures within the Finance category that you need to monitor. Usually you will have two to five financial measures.

Be sure to name *measures,* not goals or targets. Measures are numerical indicators that you graph and display to evaluate performance toward goals. They are closely related, but different.

For example, you may have a goal to

Increase sales to $10M.

The *goal* is to increase sales. *Measures* could include *sales*, *percent sales increase*, or *percent sales to target*. The *target* is $10M.

For your Scorecard, focus on *measures*.

Recognize that you may need more than one measure for a goal. For example, a goal to

Increase profits by 15 percent by September 30

may have three measures:

- *Monthly profit*

- *Profit year-to-date*

- *Percent profit increase over last year*

Brainstorm several potential measures for each goal.

Refine and Pinpoint Your Best Financial Indicators

After brainstorming and identifying measures for each goal, refine your brainstormed list. Consider the following questions:

- Is this a measure that I can count, quantify, and graph?

- Will this measure give me useful, actionable feedback?

- Is this a measure I can influence or affect?

- Will my team, boss, customers, and I care about the outcome of the measure?

Be sure you have at least one measure per goal. If you are having a difficult time determining the measure, consider rewriting the goal. You want an outcome that you can measure and evaluate.

Summarize your measures on your Path To Profitable Measures worksheet. Review the measures to ensure they will provide meaningful feedback to you and your team.

Our Case Study

Kathy, our marketing director from the television station, reviewed her financial goals and brainstormed her financial measures.

From her goal to

Attract at least six new sponsors and retain at least 90 percent of existing sponsors by December 31.

Kathy felt the measures were easily identified:

- *Number of new sponsors*

- *Percent existing sponsors retained*

However, Kathy's goal to

By December 31, keep department expenses within budget.

appeared simple at first, but she realized it was a little trickier as she identified seven potential measures:

- *Station revenues*

- *Station expenses*

- *Station profits*

- *Monthly department expenses*

- *Percent budget variance*

- *Expenses per department employee*

- *Weekly spending*

Looking closely, Kathy felt that *station revenues*, *station expenses*, and *station profits* were beyond her control, but Kathy knew that she impacted *station expenses* and *station profits* by her ability to manage her budget.

Additionally, Kathy felt that *expenses per department employee* and *weekly spending* were not going to provide much useful information.

So, she removed the first three indicators and the last two indicators, focusing on her *department expenses* and her department's *percent budget variance* (the percent difference between her budget and her actual department expenditures).

Ultimately, Kathy decided that she needed to monitor these four indicators in her Finances category, as shown in Figure 4.

Your Instructions

Examine your financial goals and determine the appropriate measures. Brainstorm, refine, and transfer your financial measures to your Path to Profitable Measures worksheet.

Good job—on to Step 5!

Categories	Station's Long-Term Goals	Kathy's Goals	Kathy's Measures
Finances	Increase net revenues	Attract at least six new sponsors and retain at least 90 percent of existing sponsors by December 31	Number of new sponsors Percent existing sponsors retained
	Develop recurring revenue streams		
	Improve profits	By December 31, keep department expenses within budget	Monthly department expenses Percent budget variance
Customers	Increase market share	Increase viewer participation in call-in shows by 10 percent by December 31	
	Broaden diversity of viewers	Host four public-relations events for at least 2500 participants by September 30	
	Establish a distinct identity in the market	Develop branding identity standards guidelines and evaluate station's efforts at maintaining standards by November 30	
Operations	Lower operations costs		
	Ensure uniformity of branding in all on-air and off-air activities	Distribute at least 10,000 pieces of marketing collateral consistent with branding guidelines by December 31	
Employees	Ensure staff is cross-trained and fully proficient in all on-air production capabilities	Have employees complete 24 hours of training by August 31	
	Increase ROI for training	Evaluate benefits from training by December 31	

Figure 4 Kathy's worksheet with financial measures.

Step 5:
Define Your Customer
Indicators

Introduction   Customers are the recipients of the value, services, and products that you produce. You must satisfy customers to reach your targets for sales and profits. More importantly, you must keep customers coming back to achieve targets for growth.

Most people, however, fall into the trap of measuring only *customer satisfaction.*

Satisfied customers may like what you offer and may even like you and your company. However, their satisfaction gives little indication about whether they will do business with you again. Even more, satisfaction levels rarely tell you whether customers will recommend other potential customers to you.[2]

There are three important questions you must ask your customers, and obtain their responses, for more profitable feedback:

- How likely are you to purchase our products and services in the future?

- How likely are you to recommend our company to a friend or colleague?

- How strongly do you agree that our company deserves your loyalty?

In this step, we'll use these three questions as the focus for the best customer indicators for your Scorecard.

Review Your Customer Goals   To keep finance results moving toward targets, every firm must have customers who repeat business and provide referrals. Your customer goals and indicators must reflect this simple reality.

If you directly serve external customers who pay for services, you must measure loyalty—the willingness to repeat business—and willingness or tendency to provide referrals.

However, you may work in an area removed from direct external customers, such as accounting, planning, or human resources. No matter, you still have internal customers that rely on you and consider the value that you provide.

You should measure the strength of your relationship and your ability to serve your internal customers' needs. You can measure this with surveys, feedback cards, questionnaires, e-mails, direct requests for ratings, or other means. I have discovered that most internal clients, that is, your coworkers and peers, are reluctant to provide direct feedback or take time to complete surveys. So you may need to consider creative alternatives, such as 360-degree feedback assessments, employee recognition systems, and informal comments and e-mails to gauge internal customer satisfaction.

Similarly, you should consider measures of external customer loyalty to see if your internal work is having an impact on the ultimate paying customers' loyalty.

Your Scorecard must reflect the outcomes you own and control. From your goals identified in step 3, let's try to identify measures for your Customer category.

Identify Measures for Each Customer Goal

Using your Path to Profitable Measures worksheet, examine your goals for the Customer category and identify appropriate measures. As before, you will have one to three customer measures per goal.

For example, you may have a *goal* to

Increase customer loyalty by 10%.

Loyalty *measures* could include:

- *Percent customers providing referrals*

- *Percent customers repeating business within 12 months*

- *Number of customers with loyalty ratings exceeding 8 (of 10 possible)*

Brainstorm several potential indicators related to your customer goals.

Refine and Pinpoint Your Best Customer Indicators

Refine your brainstormed list using the following guidelines:

- Is this a measure that I can count, quantify, and graph?

- Will this measure give me useful, actionable feedback?

- Is this a measure I can influence or affect?

- Will my team, boss, customers, and I care about the outcome of the measure?

Be sure you have at least one measure per goal. If you are having a difficult time determining a measure, consider rewriting the goal statement. You want an outcome that you can measure and evaluate.

Summarize the measures on your Path to Profitable Measures worksheet. Review the measures to ensure that they will provide meaningful feedback to you and your team.

Our Case Study

Kathy, our marketing director, reviewed her customer goals and brainstormed her customer measures.

Kathy's goal is stated as

Increase viewer participation in call-in shows by 10 percent by December 31.

Call-in shows are live broadcasts where viewers are encouraged to call in with questions and comments. Telephone calls from viewers are a direct indication that people are watching and interested. Kathy brainstormed two potential measures for this goal:

- *Number of call-in show requests*

- *Percent increase call-in requests over last year*

Next, Kathy considered her goal:

Host four public-relations events for at least 2500 participants by September 30.

She identified two potential measures:

- *Number of public relations events hosted*

- *Number of participants at public relations events*

However, Kathy thought carefully about the need to build loyalty and referrals. She added another measure:

- *Percent increase of participants at successive events*

Kathy reasoned that her job wasn't simply to host the events, but to make sure the events created excitement and interest in the community. A good indicator of growing interest would be an increase in people—in percentage and number of participants—that came to the events.

Finally, Kathy considered her third customer goal:

Develop branding identity standards guidelines and evaluate station's efforts at maintaining standards by November 30

Kathy recognized that her job was more than just serving on the branding committee and preparing brochures and flyers with the new guidelines. She had to generate interest and enthusiasm for the station to the point that people would start watching, pick up the phone to express support, or best of all, tell others about the station.

So she identified three potential measures for this goal:

- *Number of guidelines produced by the committee*

- *Number of marketing collateral pieces distributed without guidelines*

- *Number of new viewers*

Kathy thought carefully about adding the *number of new viewers* measure to her Scorecard; she knew there were other variables affecting the station's ability to attract new viewers, particularly the quality of programs.

Finally, she added it to her Scorecard. She felt that this would link directly to her customer, the director of programming, and support his efforts to draw new viewers. Together, they might be able to influence an increase in the number of viewers, an overall strategic goal.

However, Kathy rejected the measure for *number of guidelines produced by the committee*; it was not a meaningful measure for her internal customers.

She kept the measure for *number of marketing collateral pieces distributed without guidelines*, as she felt accountable to her internal customers, the station's general manager and other directors, to produce materials that promoted the station.

Kathy recognized that these two measures would be a little harder to gather, but would be the right indicators for her Scorecard. Her team would benefit from this feedback.

Kathy summarized her customer measures on her Paths to Profitable Measures worksheet, as shown in Figure 5.

Categories	Station's Long-Term Goals	Kathy's Goals	Kathy's Measures
Finances	Increase net revenues	Attract at least six new sponsors and retain at least 90 percent of existing sponsors by December 31	Number of new sponsors Percent existing sponsors retained
	Develop recurring revenue streams		
	Improve profits	By December 31, keep department expenses within budget	Monthly department expenses Percent budget variance
Customers	Increase market share	Increase viewer participation in call-in shows by 10 percent by December 31	Number of call-in show requests Percent increase in call-in requests over last year
	Broaden diversity of viewers	Host four public-relations events for at least 2500 participants by September 30	Number of participants at events Percent increase in participants at successive events
	Establish a distinct identity in the market	Develop branding identity standards guidelines and evaluate station's efforts at maintaining standards by November 30	Number of pieces of marketing collateral distributed without branding guidelines Number of new viewers
Operations	Lower operations costs		
	Ensure uniformity of branding in all on-air and off-air activities	Distribute at least 10,000 pieces of marketing collateral consistent with branding guidelines by December 31	

Continued

Figure 5   Kathy's worksheet with customer indicators.

Continued

Categories	Station's Long-Term Goals	Kathy's Goals	Kathy's Measures
Employees	Ensure staff is cross-trained and fully proficient in all on-air production capabilities	Have employees complete 24 hours of training by August 31	
	Increase ROI for training	Evaluate benefits from training by December 31	

Your Instructions

Examine your customers and market-related goals and determine the appropriate measures. Brainstorm, refine, and transfer your customer measures to your Path to Profitable Measures worksheet.

Remember, think beyond customer satisfaction—try to identify ways to know that customers are loyal, continuing to do business with you, and providing referrals.

Good job—continue on to Step 6!

Step 6:
Define Your
Operations Indicators

Introduction   You know that you must satisfy customers to reach your targets for sales and profits. And you know that you must keep customers coming back to grow your business.

Most people know that you keep customers coming back by delivering quality products and services. I am surprised, however, by how many firms fail to track the quality of their products and services. Executives often struggle with declines in customers and profits while the problem lies undetected within their own shop.

In this step, we'll develop operations indicators for your Scorecard. You'll probably notice that defining measures for each category is getting a little harder. Most people are accustomed to thinking about financial indicators and customer indicators, but operations indicators are usually overlooked and underdeveloped.

Whether your organization provides medical supplies, legal services, or new homes, there are five important questions you must be able to answer about your operations:

- What is the volume of goods or services we actually produce?

- What does it cost us to produce the goods or services (per unit)?

- How many defects or rejections are we producing?

- How long does it take us to produce our goods or services?

- How well do we satisfy customers' requirements or expectations?

In this step, we'll use these five questions as the focus for good operations indicators for your Scorecard.

What is the volume of goods or services we produce?

Start with the basics: how many outcomes do you produce?

This sounds like something every manager would know about his or her organization, but I've learned not to make any assumptions. I once worked with a large manufacturing firm that was experiencing declining sales. The firm decided to pull all the teams together from product development, engineering, production, marketing, and sales to find the problem.

We flowcharted the entire process and developed Scorecards for each area. Each team gathered data, developed graphs, and shared Scorecards.

Looking at the feedback, the answer leaped out at us: product development had not produced a single output—a new product concept—in more than 12 months. The entire process had a bottleneck at the start and no one knew it until the product development scorecard went on the wall.

So, consider the outcome indicators appropriate to your organization and operation. Start with your goals. For example, if you have the goal:

Increase the number of deliveries to customers by 15 percent by June.

Potential measures include:

- *Number of customer deliveries*

- *Percent increase of customer deliveries (rolling 12 month average)*

- *Percent increase of customer deliveries from same month last year*

On your Path to Profitable Measures worksheet, examine your operations goals and include a measure of basic production, as appropriate.

What does it cost us to produce the goods or services (per unit)?

This measure is a little trickier, as it involves some indicator of productivity. Manufacturing businesses usually have no problem, as production counts are easily tallied and expenses can be determined. The ratio of goods produced to costs usually yields this indicator.

Productivity indicators for service businesses are more difficult to determine. For example, in a legal firm, what is the real service unit—a client? a case? a verdict? For medical care, is a service unit a patient, an office visit, or a billable transaction? You need to decide for your business.

Additionally, it's hard to break out the costs for each service unit, as some accounting systems are not set up to provide the information you need.

Bottom line: consider a unit cost measure, but don't get too hung up on it if it doesn't work for your operation. On the other hand, don't give up too easily if it's the right thing to measure.

For example, I worked with a team of managers responsible for installing large business phone systems. Competitors were swiping business handily from this firm and managers wanted to turn this problem around.

We developed a Scorecard to provide better feedback on operations. (It turned out that the managers had stacks of binders packed with hundreds of indicators, but no one could decipher the reports. Data glut, information famine!)

When we dug out and presented the cost per installed phone system, the managers realized they were losing money on every installation. Plus, their costs were 20 percent higher than competitors'.

No one knew this until we assembled the Scorecard. It took a few months of concerted actions, but the managers were able to bring costs into line and compete, bringing customers back to the fold.

Examine your Path to Profitable Measures worksheet and define a unit cost measure, as appropriate.

How many defects or rejections are we producing?

Look at the units of goods and services you produce. Now consider how you measure defects.

Defects are defined simply as "anything that does not meet customers' requirements or expectations."

So, if you are a florist, a delivery that is late, spoiled, or rejected by a customer is a defect. If you are a retail manager, an angry customer leaving your store, a returned item, or a damaged item is a defect.

If you operate a car dealership, a defect measure might be number of cars not ready on promised date, number or percent of service complaints, or number of cars damaged during transport.

Start with customers' basic expectations of your goods or services. Think about what your customers require or expect from you.

For example, when a large pizza chain promises "delivery within 30 minutes or the pizza is on us," you'd better believe they are measuring the number and percent of pizzas not delivered within 30 minutes. A late delivery is a defect and it's costing the company money.

Defects cost your organization money as well, probably more than you realize. Many studies point out that firms that don't measure their defects have costs that are 40 to 60 percent higher than firms that track defects. They're a direct hit to your bottom line.

So, get your Path to Profitable Measures worksheet and figure out your measures for defects in operations.

How long does it take us to produce our goods or services?

In Scorecard parlance, the measure for "how long it takes" is known as cycle time. Again, start with the fundamental of what you produce. How long (hours, days, weeks, or months) does it take to produce the good or service?

This may not be a meaningful measure for all businesses, such as architectural firms, when customers are normally more concerned with quality over speed, or businesses like massage therapy where time is "built in" to the service. (That is, 30-minute massages can't be streamlined and delivered in 20 minutes with the same level of customer expectation.)

If, however, you produce goods and services repetitively and can benefit from shortening the time to produce your outcomes, you need a measure of cycle time.

For example, a housecleaning firm might want to track cycle time measures. An operator for a housecleaning business should be able to monitor and predict how long it will take to clean a house. There are a couple of ways to measure this, such as:

- *Average number of minutes to clean*

- *Average number of houses cleaned per day*

Regardless of how you choose to measure—average production time or number of units produced per time (hour, day, week, or month)—consider a cycle time measure.

Get your Path to Profitable Measures worksheet and determine the appropriate cycle time measure(s) for your operation.

How well do we satisfy customers' requirements or expectations?

Your Scorecard must provide feedback on whether you are fulfilling customers' expectations. Customers' expectations are defined by their *needs* and *wants*.

To attract customers, you must first satisfy the *need*. If you are delivering accounting services, your customers *need* your services to be compliant with the standards of accounting, mathematically accurate, and legible. Usually, you do *not* measure your ability to satisfy needs; you won't be in business long if you're not satisfying needs.

Satisfying customers' *needs* won't distinguish you. You must satisfy *wants* to keep customers coming back. For accounting services, customers *want* you to be pleasant, prompt, and attentive to their individual requests.

However, customers' wants vary. You must ensure that you know what they are and that you measure your ability to deliver.

The easiest way to determine whether you are satisfying customers' wants is to ask! This can be done through:

- Face-to-face interviews

- Phone interviews

- Feedback cards

- Customer complaints

- Service contracts

- Negotiations

- Custom-designed questionnaires

- Careful listening during any customer interaction

Listen carefully every time you have contact with your customers. What are they really seeking that would excite them and create loyalty: Ease of use? The best price? Superior service and attentiveness? Something unique?

For example, I worked with a team of computer service specialists a few years ago that repaired computers. The specialists tracked response time, repair time, rework rates, and customer satisfaction on their scorecard.

The specialists were very skilled and consistently responded to service calls within 30 minutes. Repairs were handled promptly and rework was less than three percent.

However, customer satisfaction scores were flat. The technicians had improved every operational indicator, but customer satisfaction had not budged.

One day, a service specialist casually asked about a customer's satisfaction with their service.

The customer said everything was great except the response time.

The specialist was puzzled, because he knew he was there within 30 minutes, as promised. The specialist probed a little deeper and discovered that the customer *didn't want* the specialist there immediately, but instead wanted to specify an appointment time. The customer had to change her schedule to meet the specialist at her office and wasn't happy about it.

In other words, the customer didn't care about the 30-minute response time promise, and wanted to arrange a more convenient appointment time. Technicians checked this with other customers and heard the same complaint.

The team modified its practices and allowed customers to specify the time for a service call. The team dropped its response time measure and began tracking its ability to hit customers' requested appointment times. The team became adept at nailing customers' requests to within five minutes and customer satisfaction soared.

The point is to consider operations measures that truly provide insight into what customers value. Think about these questions:

- Do you truly know your customers' expectations?

- Does your Scorecard provide feedback on the important aspects of your products and services?

- Does your work team know what it takes to earn customer loyalty and repeat business?

- Do the operations indicators provide feedback that allow you to generate referrals and loyalty?

Turn to your Paths to Profitable Measures worksheet and identify your indicators for the Operations category. Try to get feedback on the attributes of your goods and services that build loyalty, generate referrals, and keep customers coming back.

Our Case Study

Kathy, our television marketing director, reviewed her operations goals and brainstormed her operations measures.

From Kathy's goal to

Distribute at least 10,000 pieces of marketing collateral consistent with branding guidelines by December 31.

She brainstormed three potential measures for this goal:

- *Number of marketing collateral pieces generated with new branding guidelines (a volume measure)*

- *Number of pieces distributed without branding guidelines (defect measure)*

- *Number of calls generated from flyers (customers' expectations)*

Kathy decided that a cycle time measure wouldn't mean much for her team; they were more concerned with meeting deadlines and delivering quality marketing collateral that would elicit a customer response.

Additionally, she didn't see the need for a cost measure, as her main goal was to stay within budget, already covered in her finance measures.

Kathy recognized that her three potential measures would be a little harder to gather, but would be the right indicators for her Scorecard. Her team would benefit from this feedback.

Categories	Station's Long-Term Goals	Kathy's Goals	Kathy's Measures
Finances	Increase net revenues	Attract at least six new sponsors and retain at least 90 percent of existing sponsors by December 31	Number of new sponsors Percent existing sponsors retained
	Develop recurring revenue streams		
	Improve profits	By December 31, keep department expenses within budget	Monthly department expenses Percent budget variance
Customers	Increase market share	Increase viewer participation in call-in shows by 10 percent by December 31	Number of call-in show requests Percent increase in call-in requests over last year
	Broaden diversity of viewers	Host four public-relations events for at least 2500 participants by September 30	Number of participants at events Percent increase in participants at successive events
	Establish a distinct identity in the market	Develop branding identity standards guidelines and evaluate station's efforts at maintaining standards by November 30	Number of new viewers
Operations	Lower operations costs		
	Ensure uniformity of branding in all on-air and off-air activities	Distribute at least 10,000 pieces of marketing collateral consistent with branding guidelines by December 31	Number of marketing collateral pieces generated with new branding guidelines Number of pieces distributed without branding guidelines Number of calls generated from flyers

Continued

Figure 6 Kathy's worksheet with operations indicators.

Continued

Categories	Station's Long-Term Goals	Kathy's Goals	Kathy's Measures
Employees	Ensure staff is cross-trained and fully proficient in all on-air production capabilities	Have employees complete 24 hours of training by August 31	
	Increase ROI for training	Evaluate benefits from training by December 31	

She noted that she had already identified the same defect measure (*Number of pieces distributed without branding guidelines*) in the Customer category. She felt it belonged in the Operations category and deleted it from the Customer category.

Kathy brainstormed and refined indicators for all her operations goals, as summarized in Figure 6.

Your Instructions

Examine your operations goals and determine the appropriate measures. Consider the five critical things you should know about your operations:

- What is the volume of goods or services we produce?

- What does it cost us to produce?

- How many defects or rejections are we producing?

- How long does it take us to produce our goods and services?

- How well do we satisfy customers' requirements or expectations?

Brainstorm, refine, and transfer your operations measures to your Path to Profitable Measures worksheet.

You're on the right path—on to Step 7!

Step 7:
Define Your
Employee Indicators

Introduction   Just as you learned in step 5 that customer indicators must go beyond measuring customer satisfaction, you should know that employee measures must extend beyond employee satisfaction, too.

You need to measure employee indicators, but satisfaction measures don't tell you much. Employees may be satisfied, but are they productive? Are they producing goods and services that customers value? Are they developing value-added skills? Are they getting what they need to be productive? Are they helping each other? Do they understand how to contribute to business results?

To answer these questions, you want feedback in three areas of employee performance:

- The employee's impact on customers, especially in relation to the customer loyalty and referral indicators described in step 5

- The employee's impact on the business, such as number of sales or growth in profits

- The employee's impact on other employees, especially the ability to help others to be more productive and profitable

Most managers understand the importance of all three areas, but too often measure the wrong employee indicators. Too many measures crop up on things like "employee's willingness to change," or "employee's attitude," attributes that are difficult to measure and even harder to improve.

Instead, stop worrying about efforts and attitudes—and focus on employees' results.

Employees come with unique capabilities and strengths. You really want to see if employees will use their strengths, ingenuity, and resources to accomplish goals and achieve results.

Measuring Employees' Impact on Customers

The first step is to figure out the measure of employee's desired results in relation to customers' needs and wants. Think about "what do employees get paid to do?" Not what is included in employees' job descriptions and duties, but "what do they produce that customers value?"

For example, specialists in customer call centers are often measured on number of calls per day or average length of call. But, are they really paid to spend all day on the phone? Are they paid to cut customers off to reduce the average length of calls?

Instead, consider what call center employees are really paid to do, such as:

- Prevent customers from defecting to competitors.

- Sell additional products and services.

- Prevent customers' problems from escalating.

- Resolve complaints in a friendly, competent way.

Relate employees' actions and outcomes to the three things that are important for you to know about your customers:

- How likely are customers to purchase our products and services in the future?

- How likely are customers to recommend our company to a friend or colleague?

- How strongly do customers agree that our company deserves their loyalty?

For example, a branch manager for a bank defined an indicator for "Number of customers purchasing additional services" (for example, a savings account, a certificate of deposit, a credit card account, or other services) providing feedback on willingness to purchase.

Pull out your Path to Profitable Measures worksheet and define indicators that will provide feedback to employees on their impact on customers.

Measuring Employees' Impact on the Business

Measuring each employee's impact on the business can be challenging. The relationships are multifaceted and complex, so most organizations struggle and end up measuring abstract competencies or satisfaction.

Avoid abstractions and measures that focus on fuzzy competencies. Cut to the chase and identify what you want employees to do and achieve as outcomes. Also, focus on employees' perceptions of a productive environment and their readiness and willingness to do good work.

Research conducted by the Gallup organization with more than 80,000 managers identified twelve key questions that you should pose to employees regularly, with six questions being especially pertinent and related to bottom-line results.[3] Employees' responses to these six questions have a direct correlation with sales, profits, and productivity.

The six questions that employees should respond to are:

1. *Do I know what is expected of me at work?*

2. *Do I have the materials and equipment I need to do my work properly?*

3. *At work do I have the opportunity to do what I do best every day?*

4. *In the last seven days have I received recognition or praise for good work?*

5. *Does my supervisor or someone at work seem to care about me as a person?*

6. *Is there someone at work who encourages my development?*

Consider using these six questions as a basis for an employee indicator. For example, each quarter an engineering manager posted average ratings from his team on the six questions on his Scorecard. The ratings and ensuing discussions about scores helped the team maintain an environment of clarity and alignment toward shared departmental goals. The feedback helped the engineering manager avoid guesswork and provide the team with appropriate expectations, supplies, encouragement, and support.

Measuring Employee Impact on Other Employees

The previous six questions focus on employees' perceptions about the work environment, but you also want to make sure employees are supporting each other. Here, you should focus on three questions, again adopted from a Gallup study of nearly 200,000 managers[4]:

- Does each employee complete work in a timely manner?

- Does each employee complete work accurately?

- Does each employee perform in a positive, helpful manner?

Responses to these three questions should be gathered twice per year, with employees rating each other on a five-point scale. Sometimes known as a "360 evaluation" (indicating feedback from the full circle of colleagues around the employee), this is useful feedback to know how employees perceive the efforts of teammates.

Note again that we are not too concerned about employee satisfaction; we are interested in measuring employees' abilities and behaviors in sustaining a productive working environment.

Review your employee goals and define indicators in the Employee category that will help create a positive working environment.

Should I produce individual Scorecards?

The answer is yes—but only under certain conditions. My experience is that individual Scorecards draw attention away from team-level goals and performance. If you are trying to create an atmosphere of mutual support and collective results, then measure outcomes and provide feedback at the team level.

However, individual Scorecards are appropriate in two instances. The first is a work group that consists of individual performers where little team interaction is expected. In other words, employees do not rely on each other to produce work. I've seen this with highly technical engineering groups where each engineer was solely responsible for his or her work. Each engineer was a specialist and no team interaction was needed or expected. The group only shared space. Basically, each engineer had his or her own set of goals and expected accomplishments; individual Scorecards were appropriate.

The second instance is when you need to track individual performance for each employee to address salary, union, or performance issues. In this case, I recommend that you keep individual Scorecards confidential and only share them one-on-one with employees. Little is gained by posting individual scores during team reviews.

For example, if you're a sales manager who needs to track the individual contributions of your sales staff, you should develop and use individual Scorecards. You should share an individual's

Scorecard with him or her regularly. Do not, however, share one salesperson's Scorecard with another salesperson; you're only inviting trouble. Keep individuals focused on their own individual and team-level targets.

Be sure that each employee understands how he or she contributes individually to team-level outcomes. Use your Scorecard to communicate expectations to each employee. Make sure employees understand performance goals, areas of priority, and what they are supposed to do. This seems obvious, but I am continually amazed at the number of employees who don't know what they are really supposed to do.

In fact, research from the Gallup organization on millions of workers in nearly every industry indicates that 67 percent of employees cannot state what is expected of them at work.[5] Look around your organization and figure out the impact of two thirds of your employees wondering daily what to do. Address this problem head-on by gathering and reporting employee ratings on their impact on customers, the business, and other employees.

Our Case Study

Kathy, our TV station marketing director, reviewed her employee goals and brainstormed her employee measures.

From Kathy's goal to

Have employees complete 24 hours of training by August 31.

She determined that the measure was easy:

* *Number of training hours completed per employee*

Determining measures for the next goal was a little harder:

Evaluate benefits from training by December 31.

Kathy realized that training should focus on helping her employees produce department outcomes, namely the outcomes covered in the operations category. So Kathy brainstormed the following measures in each of the three employee areas:

Impact on Customers

- *Number of call-in show requests*

- *Percent increase in call-in show requests over last year*

- *Number of calls generated from flyers*

Impact on Business

- *Number of new viewers*

- *Number of new sponsors*

- *Employees' self-ratings on six key questions*

Impact on Other Employees

- *Coworkers' ratings on ability to complete timely work*

- *Coworkers' ratings on completing accurate work*

- *Coworkers' ratings on performance in a positive, helpful manner*

Kathy did not want to repeat the same measures in two categories, so she left the operations measures in the operations category and placed the new measures in the employee category. Her completed Scorecard is summarized in Figure 7.

Categories	Station's Long-Term Goals	Kathy's Goals	Kathy's Measures
Finances	Increase net revenues	Attract at least six new sponsors and retain at least 90 percent of existing sponsors by December 31	Number of new sponsors Percent existing sponsors retained
	Develop recurring revenue streams		
	Improve profits	By December 31, keep department expenses within budget	Monthly department expenses Percent budget variance
Customers	Increase market share	Increase viewer participation in call-in shows by 10 percent by December 31	Number of call-in show requests Percent increase in call-in requests over last year
	Broaden diversity of viewers	Host four public-relations events for at least 2500 participants by September 30	Number of participants at events Percent increase in participants at successive events
	Establish a distinct identity in the market	Develop branding identity standards guidelines and evaluate station's efforts at maintaining standards by November 30	Number of new viewers
Operations	Lower operations costs		
	Ensure uniformity of branding in all on-air and off-air activities	Distribute at least 10,000 pieces of marketing collateral consistent with branding guidelines by December 31	Number of marketing collateral pieces generated with new branding guidelines Number of pieces distributed without branding guidelines Number of calls generated from flyers

Continued

Figure 7 Kathy's worksheet with employee indicators.

Continued

Categories	Station's Long-Term Goals	Kathy's Goals	Kathy's Measures
Employees	Ensure staff is cross-trained and fully proficient in all on-air production capabilities	Have employees complete 24 hours of training by August 31	Number of training hours completed per employee
	Increase ROI for training	Evaluate benefits from training by December 31	Employees' self-ratings on six key questions
			Coworkers' ratings on ability to complete timely work
			Coworkers' ratings on completing work accurately
			Coworkers' ratings on performance in a positive, helpful manner

Kathy was excited as she looked over her entire Scorecard. She realized several things:

- This was a far better set of measures for her and for her team than measures she had tracked previously.

- Nearly all the measures were actionable by her team. That is, she felt that she could control outcomes for all except "number of new viewers" and "number of new sponsors." For those measures, she would need to coordinate with the directors of station programming and sales.

But she recognized that she played a part in these outcomes and needed to work more closely with the programming and sales managers to achieve improvements in their results. She knew that they would welcome her help and all would benefit.

She was relieved to see the "impact on other employees" measures. She wanted to encourage feedback among employees and relieve herself as the only source of evaluation and ratings for employees.

As long as she provided feedback on operational performance and allowed employees to rate each other on ability to provide support and produce timely, accurate work, she liked the idea and felt they would benefit from the feedback.

Your Instructions

Examine your employee goals and determine the appropriate measures. Consider the three things you should know about your employees:

- Are employees having an impact on customers, especially in creating loyalty and referrals?

- Are employees having an impact on the business, creating products, services, sales, and profits?

- Are employees having an impact on other employees, especially helping others be more productive?

Brainstorm, refine, and transfer your Employees measures to your Path to Profitable Measures worksheet.

Great! You're done with your Scorecard draft and well on your way toward better feedback. Go on to Step 8—we're going to look at some interesting results.

Step 8:
Mature Your Measures

Introduction   In steps 4 through 7, you identified measures in four critical categories and outlined actions to begin developing and using better feedback. Now you're ready to assemble and review your initial results.

In this step, you'll analyze past, current, and projected performance of your important indicators. You'll discover some interesting findings as you continue!

To accomplish Step 8, complete the following actions:

1. Gather available data for each measure.

2. Develop graphs.

3. Review and analyze initial results.

4. Discuss targets and projections.

5. Discuss refinements to the measures, targets, and results.

6. Define improvement actions.

Let's look at each action in detail.

1. Gather Available Data for Each Measure   If you discover that the data simply don't exist for one or more of your measures, set up a process for systematically gathering the data. Discuss the following with other managers and your staff:

- The specific nature of the data (a rating from a survey, a value derived from accounting or business systems, a reading from an instrument, a count of how often something occurs, and so on)

- How often the data are obtained

- Who will be responsible for routinely gathering and recording the data

- How you will ensure the integrity of the data (to verify that you have accurate and reliable results)

If you get stuck at this stage, call me! I can provide tips, suggestions, and examples of simple surveys and methods for gathering data. If it's important for you to know, make sure to get the right feedback!

If you need them, ample resources are available to help you construct surveys and questionnaires, so we won't delve into details here. If you develop a survey, just be aware that there are questions you'll need to work through, such as "should I have 5, 7, or 10 points on my survey scale?" or "how many questions should I ask?" My overall suggestions: keep your surveys simple; ask what you need to know; and test your surveys and questions before release.

Prepare a worksheet for your measures and fill your worksheet with your data. An example of Kathy's worksheet is shown in Figure 8.

I recommend preparing your worksheet in Microsoft Excel or a similar spreadsheet to facilitate the production of graphs and charts. Plus, you can edit your spreadsheets as your Scorecard and measures evolve.

2. Develop Graphs

If you are using Excel (or similar software) to build your worksheets, use the graph tools. For most of your graphs, you will develop a line chart.

The line chart is a familiar format, showing time (days, weeks, months, or quarters) along the horizontal axis and the value of the measure along the vertical axis. Kathy's initial set of line charts is shown in Figure 9.

	Jan	Feb	Mar	Apr	May	Jun
Finance						
Number of new sponsors	2	1	0	2	3	1
Target	2	2	2	2	2	2
Percent existing sponsors retained	Not available					6
Target	Not available					
Monthly department expenses	22.1	23.5	20.5	26.8	23.9	25.4
Target	23	23	23	23	23	23
Percent budget variance	(4.0)	2.1	(11.0)	16.5	3.9	11.0
Target	0	0	0	0	0	0
Customers						
Number of call-in show requests	34	38	44	54	39	41
Target	Not available					
Percent increase in call-in show requests	28	35	20	32	(18)	28
Target	Not available					
Number of new viewers (000)	4.3	5.1	3.2	3.9	4.2	4.6
Target	5	5	5	5	5	5

Continued

Figure 8 Kathy's Scorecard worksheet.

Continued

	Jan	Feb	Mar	Apr	May	Jun
Number of participants at events	Not available					
Target	Not available					
Percent increase in participants at successive events	Not available					
Target	Not available					
Operations						
Number of marketing pieces with new guidelines (cumulative)	0	0	1000	1500	3500	5000
Target (cumulative)	0	0	1000	2500	5000	6000
Number of pieces distributed without branding	Not available					
Target	Not available					
Number of calls generated from flyers	Not available					
Target	Not available					
Employees						
Number of training hours per employee (cumulative)	4	6	6	12	14	16
Target (cumulative)	24	24	24	24	24	24

Continued

	Jan	Feb	Mar	Apr	May	Jun
Employee's self-ratings on six key questions	Not available					
Target	Not available					
Coworkers' ratings on completing timely work	Not available					
Target	Not available					
Coworkers' ratings on completing work accurately	Not available					
Target	Not available					
Coworkers' ratings on positive, helpful performance	Not available					
Target	Not available					

As you develop your charts, make it easy for you and your team to interpret the results. Include the following on each graph:

- The name of the measure
- At least 12 periods of performance, if available
- The desired target
- Colors to distinguish historical performance, targets, different measures on the same graph, and projections

You may want to include two or more measures on the same chart, especially if they are related. Use common sense to combine measures; don't make the charts so crowded that you can't interpret results.

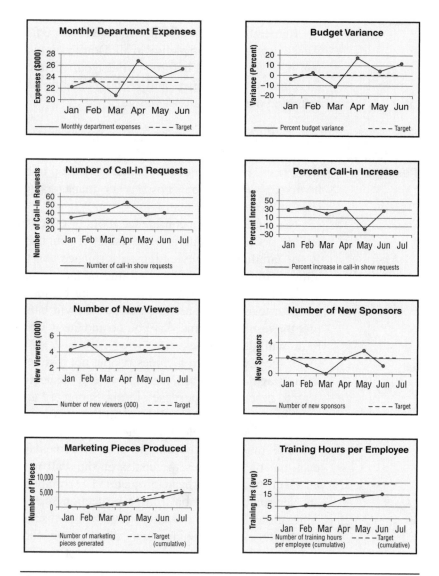

Figure 9 Kathy's initial Scorecard results (partial set).

You probably have a few measures with no historical data. That's fine; press ahead with gathering what you have and set up the processes for gathering what you need.

Remember that an incomplete picture of performance is better than no picture at all. Don't wait until you have all the data before starting your reviews. Examine what you have, and keep developing and refining your Scorecard as you go.

3. Review and Analyze Results

Assemble the team that will use the feedback provided by your Scorecard. This is probably your work team, but consider others that may need to be involved, such as your boss, other managers, or specialists from other teams.

Set aside time in a conference room or office to review, discuss, and interpret the results. If your team is not familiar with reviewing performance charts, allow extra time for discussion, interpretation, and explanation. Remember, this is important feedback for your team; do not assume that people will interpret the results the same way you do and know what to do with the feedback.

If the review team includes people not involved in drafting the Scorecard, take a minute at the beginning to describe the purpose of your Scorecard and explain how it was created. Explain that this is the first draft and you welcome suggestions.

You may want to provide printed copies for each person or display the charts on the wall with an electronic or overhead projector. I recommend an electronic display on a large projection screen. This allows the entire team to review and discuss results together, focusing their attention on each measure. However, use the means that fits your resources and needs.

For each measure, discuss four things:

- The indicator that is being measured

- The current level of performance relative to a target or expected level

- Anything unusual about performance

- Actions necessary to analyzing or improving performance

Take a moment, especially during the first few reviews, to discuss exactly *what* is being measured. Help people understand the measure so they know how to influence and drive the result. You want people to realize how to improve the number through legitimate means, not manipulation.

4. Discuss Targets and Projections

Also, you want to see where you are relative to your target for each measure. With your team, discuss if you are where you want to be, what needs to change to move toward the target, or whether the target needs adjustment.

If you don't have a target for the measure, discuss what the target should be. This is covered in detail in Step 9, Set Inspiring Targets.

Similarly, if you have projection data, review the forecasted values. Are you in line with projections? Are changing events affecting projections? Do you need to adjust projections?

If you don't have projections, discuss whether they would be helpful. Often, it's more helpful to discuss projections and "what's ahead" than to look back and analyze "what happened." Good Scorecards provide a view in both directions, using the basis of past performance to project what may happen in the future.

5. Discuss Refinements to the Measures, Targets, and Results

For your initial reviews, focus on three things: your measures, your targets, and your performance.

Your Measures

- Are these the right measures for our Scorecard?

- Do our measures tell us what we need to know?

- Do we have the right data?

- Do we trust the data?

- Are the values shown over the appropriate period?

- Do we understand what the measures are telling us?

- What do we need to do to improve our measures and our Scorecard?

Your Targets

- Do we have targets for each measure?

- Are the targets appropriate—challenging, yet achievable?

- Do we have benchmarks to compare our targets to industry and/or competitor standards?

- What do we need to do to review or improve our targets?

Your Performance

- Are we continuously improving performance and results?

- Do we see trends that make us happy—or concern us?

- Do we see unusual swings that need to be investigated?

- Do we need to celebrate achievement of certain targets or continued results?

- Do we see relationships between certain measures that need to be reinforced or investigated?

- What do we need to do to improve our performance?

6. Define Improvement Actions

From your review, identify specific actions:

- What needs to be done?

- Who will do it?

- When will it be completed?

Record your actions and distribute them following your meeting. At your next review, check progress on your action items and note those completed. Use the momentum created by identifying and completing action items to continue developing your Scorecard and your results.

Our Case Study

Kathy gathered her marketing team, consisting of four employees plus herself. She decided not to bring her boss or other managers to the review until her team had a chance to look at the results first.

Kathy thanked Susan, her administrative assistant, for pulling together the data and assembling the Scorecard charts. Susan told Kathy that she was pleased to apply her data analysis skills and hoped that the team got a lot from the review.

As the team reviewed the graphs (Figure 9), Kathy and her team noted several things:

- *Monthly department expenses* and *variance to budget* jumped around too much. Plus, it was apparent that expenses were climbing. Everyone agreed they would take actions to control expenses.

- The *number of call-in requests* climbed steadily until April, and then took a sudden drop. Kathy's team wondered if the drop was normal due to summer holidays. However, the May dip in *percent call-in increases* seemed unusual. Marketing Specialist Deana agreed to check with the production and programming teams to see if data were available from last year and find out whether the dip was normal before taking any further action.

- The *number of new viewers* was climbing after a March dip, but below overall target. Marketing Coordinator Miguel took the action to coordinate calendars with programming. With two major events coming in August and September for the fall season, Miguel wanted to coordinate the marketing message to help the station hit viewer and sponsor targets.

- The *number of marketing pieces produced* was below target. Before Kathy had a chance to question this, Production Specialist Leticia explained that a printer problem had impacted production. Kathy was delighted that Leticia had taken the initiative to investigate and report on the problem and commended her "heads-up." Leticia glowed and agreed to work with the printer to catch up on the schedule.

- *Training hours* seemed to be on track and everyone agreed to attend upcoming training sessions to hit the target before September.

Overall, Kathy's team expressed surprise and delight over the Scorecard feedback. Every individual said that this was the best picture of performance he or she had ever seen, even though several measures were missing.

Team members were encouraged and enthused over initial results. Susan, the administrative assistant, agreed to serve as the focal point for gathering additional data and preparing the remaining charts. Everyone agreed to meet again the first Thursday of August to look at July's results.

After a few announcements and an update on key calendar events, the team adjourned the meeting. Team members were talking excitedly as they filed out of the conference room.

Kathy stayed behind for a moment, smiling to herself. That was the most action and initiative she had seen from her team in a while. Would it last?

Your Instructions

Your next step—and Kathy's—is to continue gathering the data you don't yet have for the remaining indicators, and review your targets in Step 9.

You're making progress—keep going!

Step 9:
Set Inspiring Targets

Introduction   Now that you're starting to review and mature your measures, you are probably running into a common question with your team: "How are we really doing?"

You are missing data for some indicators and other indicators don't have targets. Plus, you probably don't have data to compare your performance with competitors or industry standards.

For measures that don't have a target or goal, you need to define one. Imagine jumping into a cab and saying, "Drive—and make it quick!" Without a destination, you're in for a very long and expensive ride.

The same is true with your team—you need to tell them where you're going for each indicator. So be ready to address the following questions about targets for your Scorecard measures:

- What is a valid target for each measure?

- Are we trying to achieve target or exceed target?

- How do we set good targets, especially for a measure for which we don't have any historical data?

There are no simple answers, but here are five keys for setting meaningful, challenging, and inspiring targets:

- Set positive targets.

- Set specific targets.

- Set time-bound targets.

- Set challenging targets.

- Set realistic targets.

Let's look at each aspect in detail.

Set Positive Targets

Your brain has a funny program—it ignores the word *no.* Any derivative of *no* such as *not, never,* or *don't* fails to register.

For example, imagine that you're on a diet and your spouse tells you, "Don't eat the chocolate cake." Your brain only hears "chocolate cake" and you instantly start craving some. You hadn't even thought about it until you got the message to *not* eat any.

We laugh at this odd bit of human behavior, but there is ample scientific evidence to highlight the importance of positive goals. Positive goals and statements of intent stimulate brain activity, decision making, and feelings of optimism, happiness, and hope. Negative statements tend to create feelings of fear, tension, and anxiety.[6] Your targets are derived directly from your goal statements. So make the goal statement positive and the target will be positive.

For example, you might have a goal to

Reduce all customer complaints to zero by August.

Now, your team might wonder how it's going to reduce complaints, and the goal probably won't fire people up. Your team may eliminate customer complaints by refusing to answer the phone!

If, however, you restate the goal as

Receive more than 100 customer referrals by August.

you will create more interest, thought, and action about how you're going to generate referrals. Plus, people are more intrigued by inclines than declines, so you'll create a sense of growth and fulfillment by showing, on your Scorecard, the climb toward 100 referrals rather than the fall toward zero complaints.

Set Specific Targets

Your goals—and associated targets—must be specific. Leave no doubt as to what you intend or want.

I'm always intrigued—and frustrated—by the half-baked goals I see in many organizations:

- *Increase productivity.*

- *Improve customer satisfaction.*

- *Make everyone happy.*

No wonder the Gallup organization, in research with more than 200,000 American workers, found that 67 percent of workers don't know what to do each day.[7] Just like our uninformed cabby that got instructions to "Drive—and make it quick!", most employees are just hurrying without a clear destination.

So, be specific. State the target clearly, such as:

- *Improve operations output by 20 percent by December.*

- *Achieve loyalty scores (that is, willingness to repeat business) of four or more (on a five-point scale) from more than 50 percent of customers in the next 90 days.*

- *Generate and implement 50 new employee suggestions within 60 days.*

It's scary to set goals like this—many people are concerned about failure or the consequences for falling short of goals. But to create powerful results, you must set powerful goals.

Remove the fear of consequences. Remember, be positive! Provide incentives, rewards, and positive feedback for progressing toward specific goals.

Set Time-Bound Targets

As we've seen in our examples, there must be a time element. Without a deadline, a goal is simply a wish.

Set a specific date for achievement. Create urgency and purpose with the deadline. Of course, try to be realistic with your target date, but get your team's attention with the priority.

Confer with your team regarding the deadline and build commitment for the date. Note it on your calendar and keep the target date alive during Scorecard reviews.

In addition to specifying a date, try stating your goals in the present tense, such as:

- *Celebrate 50 new employee suggestions implemented on July 30.*

- *Recognize the team for breaking our sales goal of $10M on September 1.*

Give your team something to look forward to and anticipate. Put it on the calendar and track performance toward the target. Encourage steps and milestones toward progress.

Set Challenging Targets

How many people read biographies of explorers who ventured from New York to New Jersey? Do you get inspired by teams that strive toward mediocrity?

People want and need a challenge. But people rarely set one for themselves and follow through unless they have leadership and support.

Think beyond your current capabilities—way beyond. Consider what it would be like if you didn't have any restrictions, especially the mental voice saying, "What are you, crazy?"

Best of all, talk with your team members about a target that stretches them and their capabilities. Tap into their passions, energies, and strengths.

Try a little exercise next time you're setting goals. Say that you're getting ready to set sales goals for next year. Circulate a memo to each individual asking him or her to fill in the blank, something like:

Celebrate total sales of $_____ by December 1.

See what you get back. You'll certainly get them talking with each other!

Share the results with the entire team and discuss the stretch target. People will surprise you with their willingness to try something new, to stretch beyond current performance, and their flexibility and creativity when faced with a challenge.

Let them stretch—and watch them perform!

Set Realistic Targets

Now, you may be surprised by the response you get from your team about the challenging targets, but as the saying goes, "Keep your eye on the sky—and your feet on the ground."

Set goals that people feel they can truly reach, given resources, time, and support. Discuss goals and targets together and work toward consensus on your goals. Get buy-in, understanding, and acceptance for your team goals.

Then, as you agree on specific goal statements, be sure to note the target levels on your Scorecard. Track performance and provide feedback religiously.

People starved for feedback will stop striving, so keep feeding them—through regular Scorecard reviews, praise for progress, discussions over setbacks, and continuous actions for improvement and results.

Sources of Targets

While you and your team should work together to define inspiring targets and goals, I recognize the reality that many targets are handed to you. There are four primary sources of targets:

- Corporate directives

- Historical performance

- Customers

- Industry

Following are some comments about each source.

Targets from Corporate Directives

Targets from corporate directives are usually the easiest to obtain. Your boss or the board sets targets and tells you what you need to do. It's simple!

Unfortunately (with apologies to hard-working bosses and boards), many corporate targets are poorly defined. Most corporate targets are simply extensions of last year's performance or numbers that are literally "pulled out of the air."

Worse, executives define the target and all managers get the same target. For example, many organizations define a target of 15 percent growth. They translate this to mean that every manager will generate 15 percent more revenues than last year.

The organization may overlook that some managers are poised to grow at 30 percent, while others are in saturated markets that will be lucky to squeeze out 10 percent growth.

If you are given a corporate target, examine the value closely:

- Is the target clearly defined and realistic?

- Is it a target that will challenge and excite you and your team?

- Is this an existing Scorecard measure or target?

- Can you think of realistic strategies and ways to achieve the target?

There are no easy answers to these questions. You need to apply your judgment, assess your situation, and determine what to do with the target.

At a minimum, discuss the target with your boss to ensure that you understand the target value and to determine viable strategies. As you refine your Scorecard, your abilities to determine whether this is a meaningful target will improve.

Targets from Historical Performance

As you begin charting your results on your Scorecard, you get a better perspective on historical performance. You and your team get a better feel for your target based on how you've done in the past.

Historical targets usually are easy to define, but suffer from being arbitrary and limiting.

Look at your historical performance, but resist the temptation to set targets solely based on history. You need to look outside of your past performance to know if your target has any relation to customers' expectations, requirements of the market, and top performers within your industry.

For example, I know of an organization that set a target to improve customer satisfaction by five percent each year for more than five years. Managers hit their modest targets—and walked away with their bonuses each year.

But the organization fell way behind its competitors in its ability to satisfy customer demands. As the managers watched customer satisfaction rise from 60 to 65 percent, competitors stole millions of dollars in business. The managers had no idea that competitors were getting satisfaction scores of 90 to 95 percent!

So, use your Scorecard to evaluate internal past performance, but base your targets, as much as possible, on external views and values. Review trade journals and sources of benchmark information. Attend conferences and watch for results during presentations. Talk with colleagues from other companies and gather insights.

Focus more on the future than the past. Don't settle for small gains when you need big ones.

Targets from Customers

Customers are a valuable and rich source of target information. You can obtain customer-defined targets from many sources:

- Customer surveys

- Focus groups

- Contracts

- Service agreements

- Informal discussions

- Feedback cards

- Interviews

This is not simple and straightforward. You will discover that different customers have differing expectations about your products, services, and performance. Surveys may reveal that some customers want your services now and are willing to pay a premium price, yet others will leave you if prices hit premium levels.

The important point is to get to know your customers and learn about their expectations. In fact, you will probably want to use multiple ways to gather information about expectations, such as interviews, surveys, and feedback cards.

As I noted in Step 5, look for targets in areas other than customer satisfaction. You want to set targets in the areas where customers sense and derive value, such as response time, friendliness, cleanliness, and other attributes of your products and services.

Evaluate whether you are even close to achieving customers' expectations and set targets toward expectations. Keep actions focused on targets and results that matter to customers.

Targets from Industry

A wonderful source of target information comes from outside your organization. Look to your industry to fully understand what's possible and to identify targets other organizations are setting.

Even better, look beyond your competitors for targets. If you simply set targets to match your competitors, you will never achieve a competitive advantage; you will only be playing catch-up.

Think about other businesses beyond yours that have similar or analogous work processes or outcomes. For example, Southwest Airlines maintains an advantage in its industry with its focus on rapid turnaround of its airplanes. Southwest employees know that the company only makes money when planes are in the air.[8]

Years ago, Southwest determined that it did not want to merely duplicate other airlines. To devise new ways to quickly service airplanes, Southwest looked at auto racing teams, known for their ability to quickly receive, service, fuel, and release vehicles.[9]

There's an added advantage to considering businesses beyond your industry: they are more likely to talk with you about targets and how to achieve them. Noncompetitors won't feel threatened and may be eager to share their successes and strategies. Some digging and sharing can yield big results.

In addition to contacting firms in other industries, look at reports from industry analysts, trade journals, business magazines, benchmarking databases, and other sources. Contact a clipping service and have them keep an eye open for specific targets and contacts for your measures. Data on targets are available—keep looking!

Are we
supposed
to meet
or beat
our target?

More than likely, you will encounter this question during your Scorecard reviews: "Are we supposed to just hit our target—or do better?"

Again, there is no simple answer. Your aim is to develop a consensus on your team about your desired outcome. It only matters that you clarify expectations with your team and get everyone to agree on the desired outcome.

You may find that you want to exceed targets on some measures while simply maintaining an acceptable range on other measures. You need to balance past performance, customers' expectations, industry standards, and your business goals to determine where to focus your energy and resources toward targets.

A good practice is to focus resources toward exceeding targets that:

- Give you a competitive advantage

- Reinforce your corporate image and/or values

- Highlight areas your customers have established as priorities

- Enable other parts of your business to generate value

Be careful not to overachieve in areas where there is no payback or where you create a bottleneck in other parts of the business. For example, one business that I worked with focused on exceeding targets for production and beating times on shipments to distribution warehouses.

But the company never established targets for moving products through the warehouse and making customer deliveries on time. This resulted in prompt deliveries of piles of inventory to the warehouse—that stayed there!

Are we supposed to beat the target each time or hit it on average?

This question pops up frequently, too. Once again, look at each individual measure and discuss answers with your team. Your goals are clarity and consensus so that everyone recognizes the goal line.

Use customer feedback and industry expectations to help you with the answers. A lot depends on how critical it is to achieve or exceed the target every single time or whether it's OK to vary around an average.

For example, a customer call center set a target to dispatch a technician to repair equipment within two hours. That is, the technician was expected to appear at the customer's location within two hours of receiving the call from the customer.

Customers were not waiting with stopwatches, and the company found that if it averaged two hours consistently with a 20-minute variation, customers rarely complained. In this case, the two-hour response target with a 20-minute variation target earned the company high marks for customer loyalty and an advantage over its competitors.

The call center also discovered that customers did not like waiting on the phone. The team had a target to answer a call within two minutes and discovered that hitting an average of two minutes was unacceptable.

While most calls were answered within 30 seconds, the customers on the other side of the two-minute average were waiting for nearly four minutes. Customers perceived that they were waiting for nearly 15 minutes and often hung up. The call center found that its target of two minutes for answering calls was an absolute target, not an average.

Talk with your team and determine the appropriate answers to these questions as you develop your Scorecard. You will uncover and clarify a lot of misunderstanding about targets and expectations. That's a good thing, as this feedback helps the team improve services to customers and drive outcomes for profits and growth.

Define Improvement Actions

As you continue improving your measures and feedback, always identify specific action items to improve your Scorecard, targets, and results. Your actions must include:

- What needs to be done?

- Who will do it?

- When will it be completed?

Record your actions at each Scorecard review. Also check progress on action items from previous meetings and note those completed. Use the momentum created by completing action items to continue developing your Scorecard and your performance.

Above all, keep going! You will discover that your team's excitement grows with action, feedback, and progress toward targets and outcomes. People get excited about knowing what to do and focusing on positive changes they affect and control.

Similarly, you may find that some team members get discouraged about the more difficult measures and targets. Discuss their concerns and generate ideas and actions to rally, challenge, and unite your team.

Your next step—whew, the last one—is Step 10, Boost Results. Keep going!

Step 10:
Boost Results

Introduction   At this stage, you are reviewing Scorecard results regularly with your team and continuing to mature and refine your feedback. Of course, keep gathering data for the new measures on your Scorecard and improving your overall visibility.

As your measures and feedback mature, you will notice many opportunities for improvement. Here are seven actions that will take your team's results to the next level:

1. Take complete and personal responsibility for your team's results.

2. Conduct Scorecard reviews and provide feedback religiously.

3. Use every team member's strengths and capabilities.

4. Continuously verify customers' expectations.

5. Experiment and innovate.

6. Focus actions on priorities.

7. Push beyond the measurable.

Let's look at each action in detail.

1. Take Complete and Personal Responsibility for Your Team's Results   Every effective team has a leader; your team needs and demands your leadership. Accept the responsibility and take the helm.

As a leader, you must clarify the outcomes and expectations for your team, using your Scorecard as the source of feedback. Your job is not to do everything, though. Remember to draw upon the resources and capabilities of your team to get results.

Your Scorecard gives you a powerful tool for leading your team. But you must use the tool wisely and effectively. Be aware that some employees may be nervous, intimidated, even frightened by Scorecards. The truth is sometimes painful to confront!

To calm anxieties and to encourage your team to accept and use feedback appropriately, you must:

- Give feedback that is accurate and timely.

- Praise progress toward desired results, no matter how small or seemingly insignificant.

- Strive to identify causes for declining performance.

- Listen to employees' analyses and concerns without allowing excuses.

- Identify needed actions, but resist the temptation to prescribe actions, especially for mature, competent employees.

- Discuss and learn from failures, setbacks, and significant declines.

- Never use Scorecard feedback to threaten or browbeat employees.

The last bulleted item is extremely important. Yes, you should confront individual employees about poor performance, especially when declines are apparent and the problem is directly attributable to the employees' behaviors.

But when declines are apparent and directly linked to a single employee's actions, you should use your Scorecard feedback in a one-on-one discussion to help the employee relate his or her performance with the declining results. And these discussions should be held privately, never in front of other employees.

You will find these feedback discussions—both positive reinforcement with your team or behavior corrections with individuals—empowering, exhilarating, and probably a little scary.

For some of you, this is a whole new way of managing. But your Scorecard, if used properly, will begin to unlock the potential of your team. It's a risk, but the greater risk is starving your team and never sharing feedback that will obtain and reinforce the results you need.

This is the time for courage and heart. Your team awaits your feedback. Take charge.

2. Conduct Scorecard Reviews and Provide Feedback Religiously

I'm not referring to a spiritual experience here (though some managers have an out-of-body feeling during the first few Scorecard reviews). I'm talking about diligent and regular Scorecard reviews with your team. The path to profits is paved with feedback as you continually communicate expectations and progress with your team.

Shoot for the operational improvements that are most urgently needed. Focus on outcomes that contribute to wins and gains for your team. Show your team that it's making headway in results that matter.

Stake out specific targets. Aim for ambitious goals. Go for gains that you can actually measure and control.

You will see the intangibles—morale, trust, loyalty, and commitment—improve, as well. You will see your team's energy and enthusiasm increase. Accept these intangible improvements, but keep the focus on the tangibles—measurable business results.

Encourage your team members to get excited over their goals and progress. Keep goals alive in their minds and their hands.

Consider your reviews as "time outs" in the game. For any team to perform well, it must understand what is going well and where adjustments are needed.

Deal with problems and commit to work together to solve them. Keep your team involved in reviews. Make it clear that everyone has a stake in the decisions and outcomes.

Don't let people dodge the tough issues, gloss over downturns, or make excuses. Make your team face the facts and come up with ideas and actions on how to handle performance issues—and keep results climbing.

3. Use Every Team Member's Strengths and Capabilities

During reviews, freely pass out assignments and actions. Better yet, ask for volunteers to shore up weak areas, investigate problems, and take action. See who volunteers and which assignments your team members take. Normally, do not take all the actions yourself; let your team accept accountability and responsibility for results.

Size up your team and its strengths. Look for aspirations and preferences for assignment. Help members gain experience and expertise. Watch for concerns and resistance.

Feedback and challenges have a way of bringing out the best in a team—and the worst in a team. Depending on your team's development and maturity, you may experience some "storming" as team members jockey for roles and positions. Help your team get through tough periods by using Scorecard feedback and keeping it focused on positive outcomes.

The more you draw on team members' strengths, the better are your odds of sustaining progress and keeping your team focused. Reinforce your team's willingness to use its abilities to keep moving.

4. Continuously Verify Customers' Expectations

As you continue to work toward targets, customers' expectations and priorities will change. In other words, targets will shift. As you improve results, customers will always want more!

You must maintain a watchful eye on customers' changing expectations. To do this, use one or more of the methods described earlier:

- Face-to-face interviews

- Phone interviews

- Feedback cards

- Customer complaints

- Service agreements and contracts

- Negotiations

- Custom-designed questionnaires

- Careful listening during client meetings or any customer interaction

Keep the information current and adjust targets as you uncover new aspects of your service that customers value. Tweak and refine your measures to highlight the important dimensions of delivery.

For example, I worked with a team that delivered technical products and services for an electronics manufacturer. The team measured three dimensions of service: timeliness of delivery, technical accuracy of the information provided, and percent orders fulfilled on request.

From these three measures, the team felt it was doing a great job. Requests were filled quickly and customers rarely noted technical errors. However, during a forum with the team's top 20 customers, customers complained about poor service.

Digging into customers' complaints, the team discovered three wants:

- Specialists readily available to answer questions

- Courteous specialists

- Accurate information from the specialists

The team realized that its measures focused on the technical aspects of services, but overlooked the human elements. The team worked with customers to define the right measures and to establish targets for availability (responses within four hours), courtesy (9.5 on a 10-point scale), and accuracy of information (100 percent accurate).

The team changed its Scorecard and began realizing big improvements in customer relations, referrals, and sales.

As you gather information about customers' expectations, review your Scorecard:

- Do you truly know your customers' expectations?

- Does your Scorecard provide feedback on the important aspects of your products and services?

- Are your targets set at levels that match customers' expectations?

- Does your work team know what it takes to achieve customer loyalty and referrals?

- Are the factors that customers consider important regularly updated?

- Do Scorecard indicators provide feedback to generate customer referrals and loyalty?

Examine your Scorecard and adjust measures, targets, and actions to ensure that you are getting an accurate picture of what satisfies customers and creates repeat business.

5. Experiment and Innovate

As you adjust measures and targets to align with customers' expectations, you will probably discover gaps in your performance. There will be areas where you are not meeting expectations.

Use your feedback to continuously improve the delivery of your products and services to match expectations and close the gaps. Remember, your

Scorecard is simply the basis for action and improvement.

Improve performance by analyzing your processes and streamlining your work flows. Or reengineer your work processes and create alternative flows. Or outsource certain parts of your work to others who can do the work better, cheaper, and faster.

Work with your team to continuously keep your processes moving toward customers' expectations.

Watch for—and ignore—the five phrases that stifle creativity and initiative:

- *"We've tried that before."* So what? Figure out why it didn't work last time and try it again.

- *"That'll never work."* How do you know until you try?

- *"They'll never let us do that."* Hmm, who are they? And why would they not want you to do the right thing?

- *"We've always done it that way."* Yes, and always got the results you now have—want to try to get something different?

- *"Nobody else does it that way."* Maybe it's time someone did.

6. Focus Actions on Priorities

Your challenge is to rev up your team, mobilize its resources, and keep setbacks and bad news from stifling its energy.

Maintain a strong sense of urgency and insist that others do, as well. Be the spark plug for the group. Let employees take their cues for action from you.

Keep up the pressure for productivity. Set tight deadlines. Push for quick decisions. Encourage your team to take actions and make decisions without you. After all, everyone knows the target and knows what needs to get done.

Don't get hung up with "Well, I would have done it differently . . . ." Of course you would, but that's the power of working with a team—you're allowing and encouraging others to try things their way.

Let everyone know that you can handle honest mistakes but won't tolerate inaction or heel-dragging.

Keep moving to make measurable progress. Take tough problems and chop them into little problems; keep chipping away to achieve progress. Continue building momentum toward your targets. When you hit targets, celebrate and set new goals!

7. Push Beyond the Measurable

It may seem odd that I would encourage you *not* to measure something. But the reality is that much of what customers value is difficult to measure.

As you learn about customers' needs and wants, chart outcomes against expectations. But be mindful that customers really want relationships and their emotional needs satisfied. Sometimes that's hard to measure.

Don't get so focused on your Scorecard that you lose sight of the human element of your business. Your Scorecard must provide a basic understanding of how your operation is performing, but your customers and employees have the ultimate say about your results. Continuously interact with your customers to gauge and monitor what they truly value.

As you continue, remember to occasionally pause, reflect, and celebrate your team's achievements. Working in teams is, at best, a challenge, and team members must know that you appreciate their efforts and results.

Congratulations! You have completed the 10 steps to feedback that fuels performance. I hope that you realize that your journey has only begun.

Continue down your path to greater performance, productivity, and profits through improved measurement and feedback. You'll find greater satisfaction and achievement with less stress and time spent as you engage your team's spirit and capabilities.

Enjoy your journey—and your exceptional results!

Epilogue

Since July, Kathy's team met monthly to review updates to its Scorecard. Each time, the team discussed results, evaluated progress, identified key performance issues, and updated actions. Let's check on their progress after five months, using the updated Scorecard shown in Figure 10.

The team assembled in the conference room: Kathy, Miguel, Susan, Leticia, and Deanna. As agreed in advance, team members rotated turns leading the meeting. This time, it was Miguel's turn.

Miguel kicked off the meeting with a welcome and thank-you to Susan for developing the charts, and brought up the first slide of *Department Expenses* and *Budget Variance.*

Miguel noted the steady declines in expenses and how budget variance narrowed toward the target of zero. He commented that this was good news, but asked Kathy if they were still over budget due to the mid-year spike in expenses.

Kathy explained that she reviewed the marketing Scorecard with Robert, the station manager, and Robert was pleased overall with the marketing team's performance, including budget results.

Robert was especially happy that marketing had a Scorecard and could easily track progress and show results in key performance areas. Robert noted that the marketing department finished the year well within budget variance and showed exemplary results in other areas.

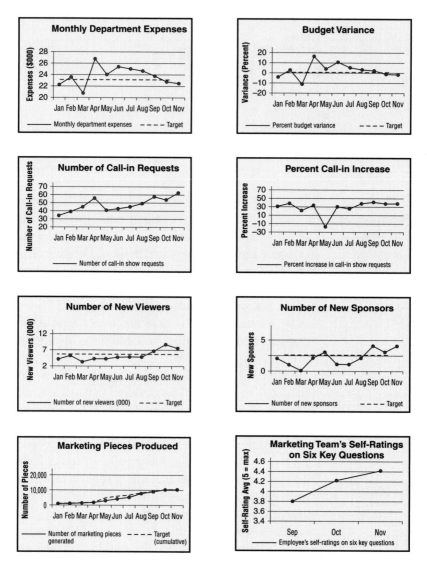

Figure 10   Kathy's Scorecard five months later.

Kathy told the team that she and Robert were very pleased by the team's ability to control expenses and manage within budget guidelines. This brought big grins from team members and a thumbs-up signal from Miguel.

Miguel continued with the number of *Call-in Requests* and *Percent Call-in Increase*, highlighting the big jump in *Percent Call-in Increase*. *Number of New Viewers* exceeded target and *Number of New Sponsors* rebounded from a mid-year downturn, which was welcome news.

Kathy seized the moment to applaud efforts that led to the results, particularly Deanna's work with the production and programming teams to coordinate marketing initiatives with featured programs in the station's lineup. Deanna acknowledged that working relations with producers had improved over the past six months. In fact, producers were asking for a peek at marketing's scorecard because they liked the easy-to-read format.

Miguel commented that his actions on coordinating calendars with other departments had paid off by allowing everyone in the station to rally around the special events in August and September for the fall season kickoff. Sponsors were pleased with the numbers of new viewers and new viewers were attracted to the new program lineup by the marketing spots. Everyone seemed happy and Miguel commented that it was the first time in his eight years at the station that the season kickoff went smoothly.

Leticia said that her actions to address the printing problem allowed her to catch up on the target for *Marketing Pieces Produced*, helping Miguel with his marketing efforts and to be ready for the special events.

Miguel reminded the team that they achieved the target for *Training Hours per Employee*, but agreed to drop the indicator temporarily from the Scorecard because team members didn't feel it was the right indicator for training effectiveness. Deanna noted that she had accepted the action to research other possible measures for training effectiveness and would report findings next month.

Team members commented on the steady climb on their new measure of *Employee's Self-Ratings on Six Key Questions*—and Kathy breathed a sigh of relief. This confirmed her belief that the team was satisfied and supported in their efforts to do good work. Deanna pointed out that the measure still did not have a target, but team members agreed not to set a target. Since it was a rating provided by team members, the target would be meaningless.

Team members also noted that getting feedback for the next three measures, *Coworkers' Ratings on Completing Timely Work*, *Coworkers' Ratings on Completing Work Accurately*, and *Coworkers' Ratings on Positive, Helpful Performance*, would be difficult. Coworkers in the station were reluctant to fill out a survey or provide any type of written feedback.

Leticia suggested that the team change the measure to incorporate the new "Star" recognition program. Recently, Robert, the station manager, had announced a new recognition program that encouraged employees to recognize other employees by nominating them for "Star" awards. Award recipients would earn a cash prize and certificate at the monthly all-hands meetings. Leticia suggested the department track the number of "Star" awards team members received from other employees, indicating their level of satisfaction with marketing services. Everyone agreed to adopt the measure for the next few months—and commit to earning a few "Star" awards.

As the team talked, Kathy reflected on the changes resulting from her Scorecard. She felt less stressed because her team was taking greater ownership of performance issues. Leticia followed up with a printer problem before Kathy had asked. Deanna was working more closely with programming and production on schedule coordination. Miguel was genuinely enthused about the outcomes from special events and had already approached her with ideas for upcoming events. Susan showed a renewed interest in her work and seemed in her element organizing the data and preparing charts for the monthly reviews.

Even beyond her team, Kathy was seeing positive impacts from her measures. Robert scheduled a meeting with Kathy to discuss the possibility of developing a stationwide Scorecard. Other managers commented to Kathy that they felt her marketing team was attempting to connect with other departments and provide support that was appreciated and valuable. Kathy even experienced an unexpected compliment from James, the engineering director, who rarely interacted with the other managers. James asked Kathy what she was feeding her team because they sure seemed to be operating on rocket fuel.

Kathy realized that her job as a manager was easier now because her team had meaningful feedback to aid decisions, guide actions, and respond to changes quickly and appropriately. The team members talked more openly among themselves and other station employees, and seemed more engaged in their work. Certainly, staff meetings were far more interesting and Kathy didn't feel like she was constantly prodding her team. Her staff seemed to mature and become more accountable right before her eyes.

Kathy was shaken from her reverie as she noticed all her team members looking at her. Miguel said, "Kathy, it looks like you didn't hear us. Do you mind if we organize a holiday party to celebrate our results? We like what we've done. And we think we can do even better next year."

Kathy smiled. "I think we can work something out."

Appendix:
Path to Profitable
Measures Worksheet

Categories	Organization's Long-Term Goals	Your Goals	Your Measures
Finances			
Customers			

Categories	Organization's Long-Term Goals	Your Goals	Your Measures
Operations			
Employees			

Endnotes

1. P. Hjelt, "The Secrets of Execution: Strategy May Be Important, But the World's Most Admired Companies Know How to Get Things Done," *Fortune* 149, no. 4 (March 8 2004): 54–57.
2. F. Reichheld, "The One Number You Need to Grow," *Harvard Business Review* 81, no. 12 (December 2003): 46–54.
3. M. Buckingham and C. Coffman, *First, Break All the Rules* (New York: Simon and Schuster, 1999).
4. M. Buckingham and D. Clifton, *Now, Discover Your Strengths* (New York: Free Press, 2001).
5. "The Four Disciplines of Sustainable Growth," *Gallup Management Journal* (September 26 2002).
6. S. Moss and J. Sanchez, "Are Your Employees Avoiding You? Managerial Strategies for Closing the Feedback Gap," *Academy of Management Executive* 18, no. 1 (2004): 32–44.
7. See notes 3 and 4.
8. D. Fisher, "Is There Such a Thing As Nonstop Growth?" *Forbes* 170, no. 1 (July 8 2002): 82–84.
9. A. Murdoch, "Lateral Benchmarking or What Formula One Taught an Airline," *Management Today* (November 1997): 64–67.

Suggested Readings

Brown, M. *Keeping Score: Using the Right Metrics to Drive World-Class Performance.* New York: Productivity, Inc., 1996. 224 pages.
Brown's book shows how to pinpoint key measures, evaluate current approaches, and redesign inadequate metrics.

Brown, M. *Winning Score: How to Design and Implement Organizational Scorecards.* Portland, OR: Productivity Press, 2000. 310 pages.
Brown provides checklists, interview questions, and other useful tools to help managers translate goals into measures. This is a more sophisticated text for managers wishing to refine existing measurement systems.

Chang, R., and M. Morgan. *Performance Scorecards: Measuring the Right Things in the Real World.* San Francisco: Jossey-Bass, 2000. 162 pages.
This book provides a storyline narrative, based on actual implementation experiences, of an executive moving his team from frustration to fulfillment with a six-step process for defining and deploying scorecards. Typical implementation issues and prevention strategies are explained.

Frost, B., and R. Frost. *Measuring Performance: Using the New Metrics To Deploy Strategy and Improve Performance.* Dallas, TX: Measurement International, 2000. 96 pages.
This primer presents the topic of measures in plain language, explaining how measures give leaders leverage to create change and produce better results. The authors cover how to use metrics to improve performance and describe issues that arise in producing metrics.

Gupta, P., and A. W. Wiggenhorn. *Six Sigma Business Scorecard: Creating a Comprehensive Corporate Performance Measurement System.* New York: McGraw Hill Professional, 2001.
Six Sigma is a widely-recognized tool to improve business performance and profitability. Readers learn how to track improvements in quality and profitability while implementing Six Sigma.

Harbour, J. *The Basics of Performance Measurement.* Portland, OR: Productivity Press, 1997. 43 pages.
This slim guide provides an overview of measurement fundamentals: types of measures, measurement displays, and measurement hierarchies.

Kaplan, R., and D. Norton. *The Balanced Scorecard: Translating Strategy to Action.* Boston: Harvard Business School Press, 1997. 323 pages.
The authors show how to use measures in four categories—financial performance, customer knowledge, internal business processes, and learning and growth—to align initiatives and processes for desired results.

Kaydos, W. *Operational Performance Measurement: Increasing Total Productivity.* New York: St. Lucie Press, 1999. 245 pages.
The book features procedures for identifying what to measure and specific steps managers can take to gather measures.

Niven, P. *Balanced Scorecard Step-by-Step: Maximizing Performance and Maintaining Results.* New York: John Wiley & Sons, 2002. 334 pages.
This is an excellent guide for executives interested in scorecard implementation across a large organization. Examples and illustrations for linking scorecards to strategic plans are provided.

Olve, N., J. Roy, and M. Wetter. *Performance Drivers: A Practical Guide to Using the Balanced Scorecard.* New York: John Wiley & Sons, 1997. 347 pages.
The authors provide a step-by-step method for introducing the *balanced scorecard,* creating a balanced view of financial, customer, business process, and learning and growth indicators.

About the Author

Mark Morgan is president of Momentum Performance Group, a consulting and training firm that helps executives and business owners achieve better results through improved measures and feedback.

Mark co-authored *Performance Scorecards: Measuring the Right Things in the Real World* and authored *Coaching: 50 Steps to Business Results.* He has published more than a dozen articles and presented hundreds of workshops and seminars on performance, measurement, and leadership.

Mark has worked with more than 200 executive teams from Fidelity, Hasbro, Nortel, NASA, JP Morgan Chase, Boeing, BellSouth, the US EPA, TimeWarner, and more than 60 other clients from government, education, and business.

Mark earned his doctorate from the University of Florida and served as an examiner for the Malcolm Baldrige National Quality Award for three years.

Formerly, Mark was the director of quality, ethics, and communication for Northrop Grumman's Data Systems Division and the manager for quality with Grumman at NASA's Johnson Space Center in Texas and at the Kennedy Space Center in Florida.

Mark lives in central Florida with his wife and three children.

Index